Schtick-to-it-tiveness

That's what Woody's got, along with comic genius and an image that's captured the hearts of the now generation.

He's the super-ordinary person who's survived in spite of himself and the rest of the world, the little guy who hit the top by being the perfect loser.

Everybody loves him and laughs at/with/after/ for him.

He is a funny person.

But what is he *really* like?

The next 176 pages will give you a clue... and not a few laughs.

WOODY ALLEN
Clown Prince of American Humor
BY BILL ADLER AND JERRY FEINMAN

PINNACLE BOOKS • NEW YORK CITY

WOODY ALLEN, THE CLOWN PRINCE OF AMERICAN HUMOR

An original Pinnacle Books edition, published for the first time anywhere.

ISBN: 0-523-00786-8

First printing, November 1975

Cover illustration by John & Anthony Gentile

Printed in the United States of America

PINNACLE BOOKS, INC.
275 Madison Avenue
New York, N.Y. 10016

TABLE OF CONTENTS

1

Flatbush Woody Gets His Start

Suppose you woke up one morning and found yourself changed into a skinny guy only five and a half feet tall, with stringy red hair? You'd enlist, right? Go to work in a box factory? Not if your name was Woody Allen, you wouldn't. You'd start cracking jokes like a professional fool, jittering around on one foot and grimacing as if you'd just come from the orthodontist. You'd buy a gross of envelopes and mail out your jokes from Brooklyn, where you had the bad luck to be born, to Manhattan, where guys like Ed Sullivan and Earl Wilson would use them in their columns. You'd run harder than any three other high school kids, and you wouldn't stop running, even when you were forty and famous, and the absolute master of comedy in the Western World.

How did it happen? Could this featherweight fellow who looks like a second-best butler when he's dressed up and a College

Bowl flunk out when he isn't, could this really be a top movie star? You bet your major film budget, he is. Since 1960 Woody has acted in nine movies, written seven, and directed five. In between, he's authored two Broadway plays, two television specials, lots of magazine parodies, and all his own nightclub material. So how does it feel to have your life story be a combination of Cinderella and Horatio Alger?

"Most of the time," says Woody, "I don't have much fun. The rest of the time, I don't have any fun at all."

Do we believe him? Well, yes and no. Nothing Woody says is ever absolutely straight, but nothing is a lie, either. If you were a perfectionist and liked to work fourteen hours a day and spend most of your nights in a sweaty little room editing film, you'd love being Woody Allen. And if you enjoyed living in huge apartments in New York, eating and wearing whatever you wanted, and spending millions of dollars of other people's money making your thoughts into movies, well... Woody's got all that, too—basically, the good life. Basically, the American dream. And mainly, the funniest thing around.

"My life is not a series of amusing incidents," Woody tells you, sitting in a comfortable-but-expensive red chair in his antique-filled penthouse duplex. The two of you are watching the pigeons land on Woody's massive terrace. Woody hates pigeons. He's tried to pop them off with a beebee gun or capture them with the avian equivalent of flypaper. Nothing works. Today the pigeons are back, like unpaid bills, to shake Woody's concentration and addle his supersensitive mind.

"The public wants to think of me as an incessantly performing grotesque. Girls come backstage to my dressing room; they think I'm going to roll my eyes and do routines and grab at them from behind. But really, my life is very ordinary. I do what everyone does—go to the movies, hang out with guys, chase girls, eat Chinese food." Fascinating. The maid brings lunch, rolling in noiselessly from the huge kitchen in some other part of the house. Is this New York, where every closet is rented out as an apartment and people sleep two deep? Is this an ordinary life? Come on now, Woody. You really love it, don't you?

"Well, you know, it's satisfying to shoot a good-looking film. I've only recently learned what that means. And writing is pure gravy. Every time I get a piece published in the *New Yorker*, it's like the first time all over again. Making people laugh can be good, too. When they're with you, they're really with you. I guess I *am* an incessantly performing grotesque. A monkey."

And you love him. You really love him. Lots of people do, especially women. *Cosmopolitan* called him the surprising sex symbol of the seventies. He's had two wives and heaven knows how many "relationships," and all this while he spends most of his time locked up in his study, writing and thinking. How does he do it? A point to ponder. Maybe, like Henry Kissinger, Woody has the aphrodisiac of power. Maybe women want to mother him. Or maybe it's just because Woody Allen clearly just digs women so much: their shape, their sound, their hair, everything. Everyone likes to be liked.

Women loom large in Woody's comedy. Most of his co-stars have, in fact, been large, looming women, reproductively well-endowed, with lots of white, shiny teeth.

"I was always trying to get close to girls when I was a kid," Woody says. "But they were always slamming the door on my fingers. I thought they were all beautiful. They were so...soft." His hands trace large circles in the air. "They thought I was some kind of dwarf."

Is it real, or is it a routine? Did Woody really have such a miserable childhood? Has he really been rejected since the first grade, when he couldn't get started with Hermina Jaffe, the girl with the phenomenally sexy overbite? Did his parents still want him to open a drugstore or become a brain surgeon? Again, fact and fantasy blend. Being a poor kid in Flatbush in the fifties wasn't a picnic. In addition, Woody, known to his family as Allen Stewart Konigsberg, was short, Jewish, nearsighted, and shy.

"My parents thought I was too grouchy and critical. Withdrawn. It's true I had a lot of anxiety. I was afraid of the dark, and suspicious of the light. My teachers despised me. I never did the work. But I mean never. It was preposterous. Did they really expect us to *read* all that stuff?"

So the girls didn't like him, his parents nagged him, and his teachers thought of him as a particularly unattractive piece of furniture. Not surprisingly, Woody spent a lot of time playing hookey. He drank coffee, went to the movies, and pretended he was Noel Coward. He probably daydreamed a lot about squeezing the more pneumatic parts of women, from Lana Turner to Margaret Dumont.

It was during those dreary high school years, with no girl friends, lousy grades, and a lot of guilt, that Woody discovered he was funny. He also discovered a deep competitive streak in his nature. In spite of jokes to the contrary ("I failed to make the chess team, because of my height"), he was athletic. He went out for track, baseball, and boxing. And he was good at them all. But it wasn't enough,

7

because he still wasn't tall, and he still wasn't making it with girls.

If his classmates thought his disparaging wisecracks about himself were funny, maybe somebody else would, too. Woody started sending one-liners to Earl Wilson types, of whom there were more in those days, all ravenous for new material. He sold so many jokes to the columnists that his name started turning up in print with fair regularity. This mention led to an after-school job, writing jokes to be attributed to men more famous, but less funny, than Allen Konigsberg. Every day, Woody took the subway to Manhattan to pound out thirty or forty gags. He usually had half of them written before he got to work. "I thought I was at the heart of show business," Woody says today. "But at twenty-five dollars a week, it was more like the gizzard."

Was Woody really so funny in those days? You judge. His first published joke went like this: "Woody Allen says he ate at a restaurant that had O.P.S. prices—over people's salaries." It's tempting to believe that a Woody Allen, Charlie Chaplin, or a Robert Benchley is a natural funnyman. But the evidence suggests otherwise. Woody Allen seems to be a serious, hard-working, brilliant, and intensely ambitious man, who is what he is because he works at it—all the time.

Woody went to Midwood High School,

across the street from Brooklyn College at the epicenter of bourgeois Brooklyn. He loathed it, and never talks about it these days, except in an occasional remark about the coldness (toward him) and mammary overdevelopment of the girls at Martin Kallikak High. You have to admit, it's a funnier name than Midwood.

Almost all of the Allen humor is firmly rooted in those Brooklyn Jewish beginnings. There's the standard line, for example, about Woody's father listening to the news while his mother knits a chicken. There's also the typical middle class progression of Woody's early life, a record that shows clearly that while there was progress, the Pilgrim's heart wasn't in it. He went to New York University, as he says today, simply because his parents couldn't imagine it any other way. He probably flunked out of NYU because *he* couldn't imagine it any other way.

In his nightclub act, Woody used to like to say that he was thrown out of college for cheating on the metaphysics exam: he looked into the soul of another boy. When his mother tried to kill herself with an overdose of Mah-Jongg tiles, he enrolled at City College of New York, and was thrown out of there, too. This whirl in the academic revolving door seems to have been the way Woody chose avoiding becoming a pharmacist and opening a drugstore. According to him, this is what his mother wants him to do, even today. But if Woody Allen's upbringing was aimed at making him believe that he should walk small and h e that disaster would pass him by, this intense competitive man has chosen instead to try to itrun disaster.

Once it was clear that Woody and higher education wanted nothing more to do with each other, he started working full-time as a comedy writer for television personalities. He went from gag writer for Peter Lind Hayes and Herb Shriner to general NBC comedy man to jobs for Pat Boone, Art Carney, Sid Ceasar, and Jack Paar. By the time he was twenty-two, Woody was making $1,500.00 a week as a writer for "The Garry Moore Show." He was also standing in line to buy tickets to the show because he was embarrassed to bother anyone for a pass.

It was about this time that Woody Allen's agents, John Rollins and Charles Joffe, decided he really should be performing his own material in nightclubs. Woody was intrigued and terrified by the idea. He had decided by then that he wanted to become a playwright, but he figured that performing would help him learn about the theater while he wrote. He also figured it would help feed him, but even he couldn't have guessed how well.

Rollins and Joffe talked a friend of theirs into letting Woody appear—for no pay—in his club, the Duplex, in Greenwich Village. Every night for a year, Woody would come downtown from work on "The Garry Moore Show" and tell jokes half the night to ten or twelve people at the Duplex. Everybody who was there, including Woody, admits that at the beginning he was awful. Of course the material was very polished by this time, after all, Woody had been a big-time comedy writer for five years. But his delivery was more like a refusal. Either Rollins or Joffe had to be there at every one of their client's performances, mostly because they were afraid he might run away if somebody didn't watch him. Woody worked at the Duplex for a year. He has described it as the worst year of his life.

He lost his Garry Moore job because he didn't show up every morning at nine to devote his talents to making Garry funny. It's no wonder, since he had been up half the night, trying to make Woody Allen funny. For the first time since he was old enough to work, he wasn't making any money. His marriage was breaking up, his act wouldn't work, and the weather was awful. It is typical of Woody that in the face of all this misery he only became more doggedly determined.

"I started out thinking," Woody says, "that if my material was funny, I would be funny."

But what he discovered was a secret that had actually been growing under some neglected lobe of his brain all the time he had been writing jokes for other comedians: the comedian who lasts is the one who creates not just one-liners, but a whole comic personality.

"What I'm really interested in, is creating an image of a warm person that people will accept as funny apart from the joke."

Once he caught on to the difference between a guy who's only as good as his next gag and the true comic personality, Woody's act began to take hold. He found himself turning into a professional, someone who can be consistently funny night after night, instead of unpredictable and uneven, as he had been at the beginning. It seems to be during this period that the persona of Heywood Allen was born, a clown in the tradition of Charlie Chaplin, a personality that was a subtle and hilarious exaggeration of all the traits of his creator.

This new American clown became so popular in the Village that the Duplex had to be enlarged. He began to get offers from other New York clubs, then from places like Mr. Kelly's in Chicago and the hungry I in San Francisco. He was invited to perform uptown at the Blue Angel, and finally was asked to come back to "the Tonight Show," this time as a performer instead of a gag writer. The comic creation was essentially complete, the little man with the droopy red hair that was a perfect complement for the Brooklyn jokes, the loser jokes, the ex-wife jokes.

Like all Woody Allen material, the ex-wife jokes were based on, and at the expense of, a real ex-wife. Harlene Rosen had married Woody when she was only sixteen years old. She has been described by friends as serious, withdrawn, intelligent. One of Woody's oldest friends also noted that Harlene had very big breasts. Woody himself at this period might well have been described as serious and withdrawn, and his abiding interest in very big breasts is a public legend.

Probably both Woody and Harlene changed radically during those post-adolescent years. For whatever reason, five years after they married, they split. "Nothing special," says Woody in a serious moment, "we were just too young." Onstage, he said, "For a while we debated whether to get a divorce or take a two-week vacation. Finally, we reasoned that a vacation is only a few days, but a divorce you'll always have." He also said some rather more insulting things about his ex, including, when told that she had been attacked and violated on the street, "If I know her, it wasn't a moving violation."

Though the breakup itself was about as amicable as such things ever are, Woody's life is his material, and the ex-wife jokes were coming so thick and fast—and on national television—that Harlene decided to sue for defamation of character. Woody never had much to say to the press about the suit, except that it wasn't a stunt, and that he'd been sued before.

"Women are always claiming I'm their ex-husband. They see me on television, and they say, 'that's him.' Even when the father-in-law says he's never seen me in his life, the women insist I'm the guy. It's weird." Just one of the occupational hazards of the famous and rich. It's not so bad. Shows you've made it.

By the time he actually got his divorce, Woody really was making it. He had an East Side apartment, a great act, and a shrink. Every performer needs a psychoanalyst. He also had the characteristic Woody Allen attitude toward his material. Anything was fair game. Some of what he said on stage was true. Some was utter fantasy. Woody never cared which, as long as it got a laugh. Does this explain why he said such cruel things about Harlene?

"I have no lasting animosity toward her. I probably wouldn't recognize her if I saw her on the street. Especially not with her wrists closed." He leans back. He looks very serious. He gets the laugh.

People who know Woody now say he isn't always "on." Funny thing, though, he sure seems to be. He's like Debbie Reynolds, who once said that when she opens the fridge, and the light goes on, she does a fast twenty minutes. The Biz. It gets under your skin. Into the blood. It's probably something in the dust that blows over the footlights. The thoroughly professional Woody that emerged from Greenwich Village obscurity could turn on the comedy as quick as a sneeze. He was a new man. A Character. A long way from Allen Konigsberg.

There can be no doubt that performing and writing—and being written about—have altered Woody Allen's personality. In his first published interviews, always more serious than most of those one reads today, he used to tell reporters that his heroes were George S. Kaufman and Mort Sahl. His feeling of association with Kaufman began when Woody was very young, perhaps nine or ten, and discovering how to use the public library. Somehow he came upon a book of Kaufman plays and started reading *You Can't Take It with You*. It's the first piece of writing Allen can remember thinking was funny.

But it wasn't just the plays Allen fell in love with, it was Kaufman himself, sophisticated, cynical, aloof. Woody cultivated what he took to be a Kaufman manner, which further aggravated his shyness and lack of communication with people. Perhaps this sort of adoration from afar served as the model for the devotion Woody feels toward the Bogart ideal in *Play It Again, Sam.* In any case, the early personality that was Allen Konigsberg was equally compounded of inferiority feelings and worship of the wildly inappropriate Kaufman mannerisms.

Whatever attitude Woody adopted toward other people and the world outside his skin, he was realistic enough to know that he could never be a performer in the style of Noel Coward or George S. Kaufman. In fact, it's very likely that he despaired of becoming a comic performer in any acceptable style until the advent of Mort Sahl. Before Sahl, the stand-up comic was a tough guy of one sort or another, with a polished, structured act building up to a big-laugh climax. But Sahl's act was built, or rather loosely hung, on a series of one-lines very much like Woody Allen's jokes, in form, if not in subject.

Certainly it was the form, rather than the content of Sahl's work that appealed to Allen. Mort Sahl had a style that perfectly fitted his morbidly suggestive name. He was bitter, sharp, highly political. Woody Allen, at least at first, had none of those attributes. Further, Sahl ultimately failed to do what Woody found out was the *sine qua non* for comic survival: he did not or could not create a performing persona. Yet maybe because of the mental doors Sahl opened for Woody Allen, he never includes Mort with comedians like Shelly Berman who, he says, have "one bomb and they're dead."

In later reports, Sahl drops out as an Allen idol, to be replaced, usually, by the Marx Brothers. But the later Woody is so much more adept at saying what people want to hear that everything has the ring of new-minted truth. To Francine du Plessix Gray, interviewing him for *Cosmopolitan*, Allen said that his heroes are, "Louis Armstrong, Willie Mays, Sugar Ray Robinson, Earl Monroe, Ingmar Bergman, and Picasso." Later he tossed in Camus. Another time, he professed ultimate admiration for the intellectuals of comedy, like Robert Benchley and Nichols and May.

Allen himself has been compared favorably to Benchley, S. J. Perelman, James Thurber, Charlie Chaplin, Buster Keaton, Groucho, and Harpo, not to mention Sahl, and even Wally Cox. Is the little Brooklyn loser overcome with the honor of being placed in such Olympian company? Not at all. While he has good things to say about each of these humorists, he obviously doesn't idolize any of them. Keaton is "cold," Perelman "narrow," Chaplin "a goof-off." He has written parodies of Ingmar Bergman and Perelman. There is even a brief joke on Eisenstein's famous baby carriage scene from *Potemkin* in Allen's film,

Bananas. This, in spite of his assertion to yet another interviewer that, "Eisenstein is my god."

This shifting emphasis doesn't necessarily mean that Allen is untrue to his heroes, but that he is growing and changing all the time. His apparently limitless capacity to absorb new ideas has allowed him to metamorphose from a wisecracking Brooklyn nobody into the most popular comedian of his generation. Like many of his idols, Woody is a mass comedian, with a face that is invariably recognized on the street, and a lean, freckled hand that is invariably implored to sign autographs. But he is not satisfied or even particularly pleased by fame. His goals, like mechanical rabbits at the dog track, are always moving away, just out of his reach. Once he attained the level of a Mort Sahl, he immediately began to shoot for Ingmar Bergman. Whoever his god happens to be at the moment, the idol is a working inspiration to Woody Allen, not someone to be passively admired. When he says that he "worships" someone, he means with pencil and paper.

Once Allen understood that lasting comedy is achieved by force of a comic personality, it was only a matter of time before the world discovered him. The vehicle of his rise to national and international prominence was an ungainly movie called *What's New, Pussy-*

cat? This formless Technicolor gewgaw featured Peter O'Toole, Peter Sellers, and a lot of women. The chief scriptwriter, and also a minor actor, was Woody Allen. He had been hired away from his New York nightclub act by producer Charles Feldman, and lured to Paris with the promise of big money. Of course, there was no autonomy in this sort of project (which Woody calls a "girls-girls, sex-sex picture") for a writer, whether it was Allen or anybody else. But there really was big money, and a chance to break into film. Woody says of *Pussycat*, "It was all terribly unsatisfying, a compromise."

But unsatisfying or not, Woody took the money and ran. As a matter of fact, *What's New, Pussycat?* made so much money for its producers that it enabled Woody to run quite a way. The noisy, blowsy picture, which was really written by a committee of big shots harassing Allen, was so popular at the box office that it gave its "author" power of a different magnitude than he had known before. For Woody, *Pussycat* was the last of what might be called "talking dog" projects, in memory of his service on "The Garry Moore Show" as half a duet with a talking (and singing) canine. Hereafter, his nonsense would be nonsense of his own chosing.

His initial success convinced moviemakers to give Woody control over his own work. He became an actor, director, editor, screenwriter. In rapid succession, he wrote or produced or starred in *Take the Money and Run*, *What's Up, Tiger Lily?*, and *Casino Royale*. During the same period, he wrote a Broadway play, *Don't Drink the Water*, which played to critical and popular acclaim, and has already become a Little Theater classic. Each of these projects, including the disappointing *Casino*, made money. And in the entertainment business, if you can make money time after time, you can do anything you want.

For a while, it seemed that Woody Allen was everywhere. He appeared as guest host on "The Tonight Show," as Broadway author and star, in the movies, on records, in the pages of magazines, popping out of your clock radio in the morning. There were Allen-endorsed shirts, gadgets, and potables fighting for our attention in the ads. This frenetic production has now slowed somewhat. Probably as a result, the quality is on the rise.

After *Play It Again, Sam*, Woody said that he was through writing, "nice, light, inoffensive entertainments that would make people laugh." Although he later made a movie of *Play It Again, Sam*, which was originally produced on Broadway, none of Woody's post-*Sam* work could properly be characterized as nice or inoffensive. *Bananas* was a much more political and topical statement than

20

Allen had ever made before. In fact, he had given politics such a wide berth up to that time that one reporter had remarked that Woody's act was unique, if for nothing else, because he never mentioned John F. Kennedy.

After *Bananas* came *Everything You Always Wanted to Know About Sex (But Were Afraid to Ask)*, based on the title, and not much else, of Dr. Reuben's phenomenal best-seller. This picture, almost Bosch-like in its extreme grotesqueness, is perhaps the most *outré* big Hollywood film ever made. The film that included the surrealistic Big Breast was followed by *Sleeper*, the story of the Allen persona (who might be called, by analogy to Chaplin's Little Tramp, the Little Drip) drawn against his will into social commentary and action.

By this time, Allen had shot through the middle class and arrived in the realm of the really rich. His income included $3,500 a week from royalties on *Don't Drink the Water*, $75,000 for doing whatever it was he did to *What's Up, Tiger Lily?*, not to mention guest appearances on TV at $10,000 a spot, and $25,000 a week whenever he felt like spending a little time in Las Vegas. The outcome of Harlene Rosen's suit against her ex-husband is lost in the mists of journalistic history. But whatever the settlement was, Woody could afford it.

Like lots of his fellow tycoons, including the richest man in the world, J. Paul Getty, Woody claims all his money doesn't give him the feeling of being rich. He likes to spend money on the things he enjoys, but there is very little extravagance in his life. He travels, collects paintings, gambles a bit when he happens to find himself where gambling is legal. He says he'd like to own a Monet, but thinks the prices are just too high. If he owns a real luxury item, it is his duplex apartment in Manhattan, where enough space to stand up in is considered upper class. Woody's particular space is more than enough to stand up in, and what's more, the apartment has been reoriented, remodeled, and redecorated as if it were the last bride on earth on her wedding day. And if you think all this doesn't cost money, consider the classic Allen joke, "Not only is God dead, but try getting a plumber on weekends."

During the period when Woody Allen's rising star became a flashing comet, he met and eventually married actress Louise Lasser. You've seen her on dozens of television commercials, as Woody's girlfriend in *Bananas*, and as his wife in *Everything You Ever Wanted to Know About Sex*. Louise Lasser is funny, intelligent, pretty, and sexy, but the marriage only survived a few years. The explanation, according to Allen and many of his friends, is that he is a perfectionist. His taste is apparently so exquisite that he cannot live with a less-than-perfect woman, or at least not for long. Of course, this fastidiousness is absolutely necessary to a man whose work is always swaying on the border between the hilarious and the revolting, the comic and the merely offensive. But if Woody has developed a warm and lovable public persona, his private self is still deeply in the thrall of the snooty shade of George S. Kaufman.

Whatever the causes of this second divorce, it was a truly amicable one. Louise is still a good friend to Woody and his new woman friend, Diane Keaton, with whom he has kept steady company for the last several years. Diane played Woody's best friend's wife in *Play It Again, Sam,* as well as the object of his devotion in *Sleeper*. His relationship with Keaton is one aspect of his life that Woody and his friends never talk about in public. The liaison is treated with a delicacy almost rivaling that of the legendary Duke Ellington, who once asked a friend to book a hotel room for "the young lady who is traveling parallel to me."

There is a whole side to Woody Allen's character that has no part in his public life. Of course, it's right there in front of you, if you think about it. But the Allen persona encourages us not to think about it. Woody the performer is a loser, a little guy who's always scurrying one step ahead of life's big boot. But Woody the person has been almost monotonously successful. Think of it: he was a professional comedy writer at the age of seventeen, if not actually at the heart of show business, at least close enough to hear the beat. Where were you when you were seventeen? He was a millionaire by the time he was thirty, a comic immortal before he was forty. The only thing Charlie Chaplin has on Woody is knighthood.

Even those early, unspeakable days in Flatbush weren't so devoid of triumph as the Little Drip would like you to believe. It is rarely mentioned, for example, that Woody played regular second base for the Police Athletic League in Brooklyn. As any New Yorker or baseball fan can tell you, the PAL was probably the equivalent in Brooklyn in those days of Class-A professional ball anywhere else. Remember, these were the golden years of New York baseball, when the Dodgers, the real Dodgers, were still playing at Ebbets Field. Besides that, Allen was a good enough featherweight boxer to qualify for the Golden Gloves championships. During the same years, he taught himself to play the saxophone, eventually switching to the clarinet, which he has faithfully practiced two hours a day ever since. Recently, he has begun performing with a Dixieland band, very straight, very traditional, very good New Orleans-style jazz.

Allen Stewart Konigsberg was a first-born Jewish son. If you don't think that's a big deal, you must not be one or know any. Maybe the reason he never seems impressed with his extraordinary success is that he has always known he was somebody special. If he felt inferior, it was to some remote ideal that he was expected, and expected himself, to live up to. If he plays down his success and plays up his ineptitude, it's because he's smart enough to know that all of us find it easier to identify with, and laugh at, a failure.

But the Little Drip is a creature invented by Woody Allen, not his life. His woebegone sexual fantasies we can have in abundance, his love life is none of our business. All his fears are spread out for our delectation in every Woody Allen movie, but where in his work do we ever hear about the "little lion" who stood in front of a microphone night after night at the Duplex, telling his jokes to twelve tipsy revelers who didn't laugh? In short, the work of Woody Allen is not the same thing as the life of Woody Allen, as any good critic could have told you at the start. The extent to which you believe it's the same is merely a measure of Woody's skill.

According to John Jay Chapman, the heart

of the world is Jewish. If this is true, the world has a lot in common with Woody Allen. For the heart of Allen's persona, the Little Drip, is that everlasting outsider who figures so largely in Jewish tradition. The Drip is always a newcomer, earnestly trying to master a surpassingly strange environment by the force of his wit. Although the Little Drip is often referred to in magazines as a *schlemiel*, or even, God forbid, a "schlepper-chaun" (at least twice) the character is not really a total loser or a winner, either. The Drip is really a striver, an overachiever. What makes his striving funny is the gross discrepancy between the raw material he has to work with and the ambitious finished product.

This comic distance between the real and the ideal was pushed for all it was worth in the formative years of the Little Drip. "As a boy," he says, "I was ashamed to wear glasses. I memorized the eye chart, and then on the test they asked essay questions." He would claim that he had wanted to be an FBI man, but you had to be five foot seven and have 20-20 vision. Then he decided to become a master criminal—but you have to be five foot seven and have 20-20 vision for *that*. These days, the Little Drip appears less and less as the alter ego of Woody Allen and more often as self-contained movie characters like Virgil Starkwell and Fielding Mellish (played by Woody Allen).

Man as hapless little bug is an old character in Jewish literature, both funny and serious. Even though Woody Allen continually invites comparison between himself and great men—the Marx Brothers, Chaplin, Bergman—his central creation, the comic persona, has a lot in common with the characters of men he never mentions. Possibly because it doesn't occur to him, or because it's too close for comfort, Woody never suggests that he's like Philip Roth or Norman Mailer. Well, these guys are Brooklyn Jews (Roth is from Newark, but it's the same thing), just like Woody. They're comic writers, just like Woody. Maybe they've been a little puffed up by the critics. Maybe Woody has been, too. Woody is a saloon comedian who'd like to be a serious writer. Mailer is a writer (is he serious?) who'd like to be taken seriously in the saloons. Roth is a comic writer who gets ludicrous when he's too serious.

The Little Drip gets a lot of his laughs through a hilarious misreading of reality. It's very New York, very Jewish. "Why are our days numbered," he asks, "instead of, say, lettered?" It's like something out of Kafka or Beckett.

"I really admire Beckett. I can't tell you how

much. When I was in Paris the first time, filming *What's New Pussycat*, I got to meet him. Just for a minute. He was sitting in a cafe. What a thrill! It was the only good moment in those whole six months."

Woody won't admit the comparison between himself and the great Beckett. Maybe the idea awes him. But Woody, in his way, is an absurdist, too. To the Drip, the rules of the game are sometimes as incomprehensible as they are to the people in Beckett's plays. An Allen character, for example, was expelled from college for immoral conduct: "They caught him trying to immerse a dwarf in tartar sauce."

Like everyone always says, Woody-the-Drip is a pawn of fate. But unlike Beckett characters, he's a fighter. If he's God's little chess piece, he's not just a motionless dummy. He's active, a pawn who can argue, debate, tell jokes. In spite of what the Little Drip says, he knows that God isn't dead. The malevolence of the universe has a very personal quality. God is still very much alive, and busy kicking Woody Allen around.

Perhaps it is this comic religiousness that makes the Woody Allen persona so Jewish. "Years ago, my mother gave me a bullet. I put it in my breast pocket. Two years after that I was walking down the street when a berserk evangelist heaved a Gideon Bible out a hotel room window, hitting me in the chest. That Bible would have gone through my heart, if it hadn't been for the bullet." As Elie Wiesel says in his book, *Souls on Fire*, one may be Jewish with God, in God, and even against God, but never without God.

Observers have often commented that self-deprecating humor is a thinly disguised deprecation of others. Most of our comedians have been men fairly boiling over with hate. Think of James Thurber, Bob Hope, Sid Caesar, Jackie Gleason, Mort Sahl, Shelly Berman, and most of all, Lenny Bruce. If they sometimes made fun of themselves, we didn't really believe it. It was other people (the wife, the mother-in-law, the system) who were responsible for their troubles. Woody has his hostility quotient, too, and puts a great distance between himself and other people. Yet somehow his humor, even at the beginning, offended almost no one.

The secret of this achievement most likely lies in the creation of a more complete comic persona than was usual for the cabaret circuit. It was like Chaplin's Little Tramp. When Woody Allen (Allen from Midwood?) makes fun of himself, he's making fun of a character, a creation of the author, Woody Allen.

Woody's character was the Little Drip. We liked him, we laughed at him, we thought he was a little like us. He dug girls, hated their boyfriends, got sand kicked in his face at the beach by the muscleman. Oh, yeah. We know about that.

"I went to Vic Tanny's once," Woody tells you. "This was a long time ago. I pushed and sweated and lifted and heaved for two weeks. Nothing. So I figured, why not just give Vic Tanny the money, and let him walk me home at night?" Right. We've been there, or almost.

Most of all, Woody's character was about sex. Nervous sex. Fantasy sex. Trying to impress girls with big breasts. Get them stoned. Tell them jokes, bowl them over with his intelligence, bowl them over any way at all. The Little Drip loved sex. He loved girls. Girls didn't love him. That was the whole thing, right there. Woody was playing the subject of sex like it was a virtuoso clarinet solo. Nobody ever said so much on stage before about how scary sex can be. Sometimes, Woody seemed just plain tired from chasing so hard. It turned out he wasn't the only one.

The Little Drip was at the top of his form during the years when Woody got the big push from *Playboy* and *Esquire*. *Playboy,* especially, couldn't get enough of Woody's eager, droopy face posed next to a big pair of knockers. It was the best thing that could have happened to his career. Fear of failure with the opposite sex turned out to be something everyone could relate to. Like Woody, we all suspect that maybe we're doing it wrong. We all wonder if maybe there isn't some position, some orgasm, or some *body* that's bigger and sweeter and better than the ordinary stuff we've been getting. Is Woody getting it?

"Women are a mystery to me," he says, his looking a lot like "the Immoral Mr. Teas." The luscious lady who lives with him strolls through the room. She is wearing shorts. A mystery.

Woody talked openly about sex. That's like Freud. Woody made us laugh about sex. That's not like Freud. After a while, it got so Woody just had to step out on stage next to a well-built lady and people would laugh. Woody played it for all it was worth. He posed for *Playboy* and *Esquire* with everyone from Ann-Margret to Natividad Abascal. (Who? Remember the dark-haired revolutionary girl in *Bananas*? The one who was about six feet tall and wore hardly any clothes? Right. Natividad Abascal.)

Sex jokes, God jokes, existentialism jokes, it's no wonder Woody got a reputation for being a little man with a big anxiety. It's no wonder the press called him "cerebral." But that's what's funny to Woody, and to a lot of other people too. Many of us had to sit through courses with names that could have been

"Truth 101," just like Woody did. Frankly, most of us didn't do much better at the old college grind than he did, either. That stuff *is* funny. When *Time* magazine announces that God is dead, what do you do except laugh?

So here comes Woody Allen out of Brooklyn, by way of NYU, and he's a little like Charlie Chaplin and a little like Mort Sahl and a little like even Milton Berle. He looks like us, only a little shorter. He's nervous, like us, only a little more. He's a throbbing blob of ego standing up on the nightclub stage and quivering out his insecurities. And man, is he funny. We laugh at him, we laugh at ourselves, and we feel better. God may be dead, but Woody Allen is alive and well and appearing at the Village Gate.

Early in his career Woody denied that he was an intellectual. Not "fey." Not "cerebral." Not a "librarian." He denies it still.

"I read a lot. I don't like to, but I have to. A writer has to read."

Well, a lot of university-types like Woody, but so do a lot of nonuniversity-types. One thing's sure, has been from the start, Woody Allen isn't afraid to make fun of anything. Nothing snows him. Nothing is too serious, too big. What a relief it is to chuckle about sex, roar about Jewish mothers, even have a laugh or two at the expense of absurdity. Flatbush Woody had a handle, and he used it like a trapeze.

In a few short years in the sixties, Woody soared up out of obscurity in the Village into the best rooms in America, and out the front door into movieland. From there, it was an easy glide to big director, Broadway author, parody writer, even classic in his own time. Still, we don't begrudge Woody anything. He's still one of us, and we're glad to see him make it. He looks a lot like you and me, and look how well *he's* doing. It cheers you up.

At heart, Woody is still a saloon comic. Tough enough to make it in the smoke-filled rooms and still keep his vulnerability. This is where it all started, a nightclub baby. Flatbush first, the world after. But in between, in the formative years, life was a cabaret.

2

The Nightclub Years

"Ladies and Gentlemen, we are *moderately* proud to present...Woody Allen!"

He trots out on stage, all tangled hair and tangled nerves. The audience is already laughing. They know him by now. Usually, they even know most of the jokes. The start of recognition. Oh, yeah, the little-man-against-the-elements. Playing the main rooms at Vegas.

"I hate my shower," he tells them. Titters. "It hates me too, but I hated it first." Guffaws. Always stressing his littleness, the littleness of his whole background.

"My parents," he says, holding up a tiny scrap of paper about the size of a preinflation postage stamp. "Actual size. They were really obscure. Very poor. I wanted a dog, but they were too poor to buy one, so they got me an ant. I called him Spot." They're laughing for real now, great rolling waves. Woody could tell them anything, or nothing. They even laugh when he just stands there. He has arrived.

The beginning of that phenomenally successful act was years earlier, when Woody got his first gag-writing job. He wrote jokes after school for press agents. After two years on the job, he had tossed off about 20,000 one liners for the agent to plant in the newspaper columns. "I don't remember one," he says today. "They were all necking-in-the-parking-lot jokes." But the act got started there, just the same. By the time he actually went on a stage by himself, Woody had terrific material. All homemade. Toiling away as an anonymous hack had its long-range rewards. He went from high school wiseguy to professional comic by way of those hours at the press agent's typewriter. The gags may embarrass Woody now—he definitely would not be happy to see them under his by-line—but probably he remembers a lot of them. But he was a kid then, raw, just getting a start. As a polished solo performer, it pays Woody to forget most of his early work, at least in public. Still, you know where his roots are. They're in all the years of churning out one-liners for Sid Caesar, Art Carney, Peter Lind Hayes, Herb Shriner, Carl Reiner, Mel Brooks, Garry Moore, Pat Boone, etc., etc. Woody learned from it all. From the talking dog duet he had to do for Garry Moore, from the deadlines, from the pace, from the pressure. When he finally left Garry Moore, Woody was a seasoned professional with a mind of his own. He wanted to do his own material, instead of having it cut to pieces by somebody else.

"I'd hand in sketches on that show, and they'd say, 'We don't want to mention Krushchev, because he's the leader of the slave world.' They preferred to do sketches where Carol Burnett falls down."

Why hadn't he thought of performing his own stuff before?

"I thought there was nothing to it. I thought if the material was funny, it didn't matter whose mouth it came out of. When I finally caught on that nobody could do my stuff right except me, it scared the hell out of me."

Woody mentioned his new insight one night over coffee to his manager, Charlie Joffe. Joffe wouldn't let him forget it.

"He hounded me. I should go onstage. Finally, I said, why not? If they laughed when Garry did it, they'll laugh when I do it. I still thought, even then, that what counted was having funny material. I didn't know the first thing about delivery. I fell so flat you could hear it on Morningside Heights."

It's true. Everybody in the business remembers how terrible Woody was. But he stuck. He worked like a mule. The jokes were there, and they were funny. Pretty soon Woody was funny too. He shaped the jokes to his character and his character to the jokes, until they were indistinguishable. Did he look like a librarian. Okay. The library joke:

"One day, a lot of cars pulled up around my house. They shined in searchlights, and I heard a voice over a loudspeaker say, 'We have you surrounded. This is the New York Public Library.' They wanted me to throw out *A Tale of Two Cities* and come out with my hands up. They drove me down to the main branch and took away my glasses for a year."

The Little Drip is born. And with him, a star of major magnitude. Woody had found his handle. He was the bookworm. The intellectual. The little twerp who wants to be an archcriminal but is too short. This is ironic, when you think about it. There was probably never another kid in the history of Midwood High who opened a book less often than Woody. But, a bookworm he looked, and a bookworm he became.

"People tend to be aware of their faults more than their attributes," Woody says. The Little Drip leaned on his faults as if he had nothing else. He cultivated an appearance that deliberately pointed up his smallness, his nearsightedness, his vulnerability. The heavy black horn-rimmed glasses Woody wears today are the same style he's had for fifteen years. They're as outdated as the Kingston Trio. While the world is in John Lennon spectacles, Woody sticks to his hornrims. The Little Drip can't look trendy or hip.

The Drip is eternally young. He's more vulnerable that way. The press still refers to Woody Allen as a "nice, serious boy," or a "Brooklyn boy," or just a boy. They all concur that he looks just like an undergraduate at a second-rate university. He's going on forty-one, and he's losing his hair, but he has us all completely convinced that he still looks eighteen. Or younger. He reminds us of our ancient schoolyard scorn for the square, the grind. Over the years, we Americans have suspected that anybody who reads much is a little bit weird.

And Woody built on that tradition. Before he even opened his mouth on stage, people were laughing at the way he looked. Not at first, you understand. The look took time to perfect. But once he finally got it down, he didn't change. Here's how Woody Allen looks today, onstage and off:

Saddle shoes, battered. Toes scarred from shuffling feet. Jeans. Old, but not hip-old. Just *used*. Pullover sweater dangling under a freckled, young-old face. Face like a dog whose master had just left him at the pound. Indescribable hair. "Rust-colored." "Mud-red." "Russet." Also, it's wispy, tousled, receding, looks like it has been dried in a wind tunnel. "Hangs around his neck like a setter's ears." A Jewish Setter.

All this is a healthy distance from the way Woody looked when he started out in the Village. The hornrims were in fashion then, the hair was short, and he often wore a suit and tie. He could almost pass for a bright young advertising executive. He looked much less innocent then, much more manic. He wasn't the type to wear a pullover sweater. It was too slick. The suit and tie had to go. Bring on the sweater and the funny jeans and the Scotch tape to keep the eyebrows raised in perpetual bewilderment.

So Allen Konigsberg became a saloon comedian. He hugged the mike and hammered away at his own inadequacy. He was Exhibit A in the case to prove his own drippiness. He often looked like his featherweight frame would collapse if he let go of the microphone. His natural coordination and athletic bent were concealed by worsening posture and jerky movements that made you afraid he was going to fall down. And he let you know that, if he looked like a loser, it was all in the family tradition.

"My grandfather," he would say, "was a very insignificant man. At his funeral, the hearse followed the other cars. It was nice, though. A catered funeral. They had a replica of the deceased in potato salad."

Another one: "My parents were very old world. They come from Brooklyn, which is the heart of the Old World. Their values in life are God and carpeting."

When critics picked up on Woody, they were fond of saying how different he was from the old-style, hostile stand-up comics. But secretly, we all know that there never lived a little loser from Brooklyn who wasn't harboring a lot of hostility. Audiences must have sensed, even while they were enjoying their fictional position of superiority over the Drip, that he could be bitter, too. The Press was right in more ways than one when they compared Woody to Mort Sahl and Shelly Berman.

Woody has always been open in his admiration for Sahl, less so for Berman. But he is much more likely to compare himself to Groucho and Bob Hope, those past masters of snide insecurity. The Little Drip only looked like Sahl or Berman. He was rumpled and informal, even in his earliest days when he still appeared on stage in a jacket and tie. His material, delivered in a nervous, low key, unstagy voice, seemed to be extemporaneous. But the act was really a close cousin to Hope's, both in its pacing—laugh after laugh to keep the audience off balance—and in its reliance on an unchanging comic persona as a vehicle to carry all the gags.

In the beginning, the Little Drip leaned heavily on the insecurity. He cowered and cringed, resenting it all the while, just like Hope, ungraciously losing the beautiful woman to Victor Mature. While he was mainly a cabaret performer, Woody never allowed his humor to develop a strong aggressive component. In his more recent movies, like *Sex* and *Sleeper*, a little of the snotty Woody Allen is starting to emerge. In *Sleeper*, Miles Monroe, played by Woody, actually wins the girl at the end. At this point in his growth, the character just isn't the Little Drip anymore.

But during the years of Woody's nightclub act, and even now, should he happen to perform as a stand-up comic, the man on stage was always recognizably The Drip. So where was all that hostility, that aggressiveness. It was subtle, but it was unequivocally there. If critics and reporters chose always to write him up as the complete wimp, Woody didn't care. He has never cared much for the opinions of critics, except insofar as they affect his financial success. The publicity from all those "little loser" stories in places like *Time* magazine never hurt Woody a bit at the box office.

When he was the Little Drip, Allen's

hostility was directed primarily, though by no means exclusively, against himself. This inner-directed aggressiveness—"I'll beat me up before you can do it"—is really a convoluted kind of self-defense. It's like the old joke about housebreaking a dog, who finally learns to pee on the rug, hit himself with a rolled-up newspaper, and throw himself out the back door. Woody Allen's self-flagellation has the quietly triumphant twist that, after the whipping is all over, the victim can make people laugh about it.

The Drip, even at his most abject, was always the kind of guy who would come down hard on his tormentors, if only some fairy godmother would make him seven feet tall. Woody has often said that if he had the chance to become Earl Monroe or Walt Frazier, he wouldn't hesitate a minute. Significantly, he would not be interested in being transformed into George S. Kaufman or Bob Hope, however much he may admire them. If you have the benefit of a fairy godmother, why not get yourself metamorphosed into the hippest, coolest, most powerful, and, by the way, *tallest* guy around? Unlike Lenny Bruce, whose "kidding" of people like Wilt Chamberlain was as vicious and envious as it was hip, Woody seems to have no hostility for those black athletes and musicians to whom he gives his undivided hero-worship. He has done parodies of all his other "idols," from Kierkegaard to S. J. Perelman, but as a musician or a sports enthusiast, he is absolutely serious. Woody Allen, no matter how ambitious he may be, is a man who can discern and accept his limits. Lenny Bruce was a Brooklyn boy who thought he could reshape Jewish humor into the key to the Kingdom of Hip. Woody knows better.

Yet in a different way from Bruce, Woody knows he's an outsider, and he, too, resents it. As much as he wants beautiful women, so much does he hate them for dumping on him. Hence the once-inexhaustible jokes at the expense of his ex-wife. As much as he wants and needs the helpless hilarity of his audiences, so much does he detest them when they fail to respond. In his early days as a comic, he once told an audience that if there were a prize for the worst bunch of spectators in the world, they'd win it. Another time, he turned his back on a cold-fish audience, and told his jokes to the wall. He will go out of his way to avoid encountering a group of teen-aged boys, who, he says, are the group that like him the best. (Woody, as a teen-ager, was a movie addict and an "insane" fan of Max Shulman.)

Who else is this gentle gnome hostile to, besides himself, his women, and his audience? Only other men, God, and the universe. His Mom and Dad jokes, for example, have always suggested resentment of his parents' failure to accept him. "My mother speaks to me once every two years, and asks me when I'm going to open a drug store." "See this watch?" he'll ask an audience. "My grandfather, on his deathbed, sold me this watch." Then there are the kidnapping jokes. The kidnappers, "drive me off and they send a ransom note to my parents. My father has bad reading habits. He gets into bed that night with the ransom note and he reads half of it and he got drowsy and he fell asleep." In another kidnapping routine, the Woody-character sends a ransom request to his parents with this P.S.: "This is no joke. I am enclosing a joke so you will be able to tell the difference."

The only member of his family Woody seldom jokes about, or mentions at all, is his sister, Letty. Considering that Letty is eight years younger than Woody and evidently has always worshipped him, this isn't surprising. Allen once told a reporter, "I am an only child. I have one sister." As a psychological truth, the statement is profound.

It's easy to see, once you think about it, that Woody Allen, like all funnymen, is deeply angry. On stage, the anger is, indeed, more like Bob Hope's sneaky aggression than the direct and active bitterness of Mort Sahl. Though Woody's young fans, the ones who congratulated him for not performing on Vietnam Moratorium Day, probably dislike the comparison, the similarities are many and real. Hope, in latter days, has become a sort of right-wing institution—richest performer in the world, builder of troop morale, friend of (sometime) vice-presidents. The difference in their politics makes one forget how alike these two comic characters are. Hope, too, is a cringer, a womanizer, a man whose fears and vanities are almost as big as his talent. Since he was in the habit of letting his snide remarks escape as asides to the audience, it was easier to see the bitterness in Hope than in Allen. But both men, as comedians and as people, are partial-paranoids who see gigantic forces trying to personally do them in. For Hope, it's the Commies and the weirdos. For Woody, it's the absurd universe and that ultimate kick in the groin, death.

The early Woody Allen was much too cowardly to let his hostility escape in any way. In those days, he was still trying to sublimate it all; to turn the psychic maulings suffered in childhood into show-biz gold. "If I got beat up when I was a kid," he once told an interviewer, "or got in trouble with the cops, I'd be scared, petrified. But I always knew I could be funny about it the next day. I could always make people laugh." Another time, he said, "Everything good I've ever written has been the result of a sharp, searing blow. I smash my occipital area with a heavy mallet, then write down whatever comes. I do it for the money." This latter joke contains nearly every identifying element of Woody's humor, at least through the Little Drip phase. It has hostility, self-directed; it has that grain of autobiographical truth, covered with layers of pearly exaggeration; and the surreal quality, so often remarked on, that makes people expect Allen to be an utter madman when they meet him.

Woody's surrealism consists mostly in using *non sequiturs* with such skill that his audience is persuaded to go along with the premise. This skill developed very early in Woody's evolution as a gag writer, especially when he got the chance to write for someone like Hope, who had a distinct comic personality, or an actor-comedian, like Sid Ceasar, who could assume a personality. But it wasn't until he began to perform his material himself that it was really done right. Woody, no matter what he writes—Broadway plays, movies, club routines, parodies—writes only about Woody. Since plays demand sustained character acting, other actors may come off better than Woody, as in *Don't Drink the Water* or *Play It Again, Sam,* but only Allen can do an Allen cabaret routine.

Once he did step out from behind the "safe,

warm typewriter" and into the spotlights of a nightclub stage, a whole new comic character came into being. If he delivered the jokes in a jittery, offhand style similar to improvisational comics (Nichols and May, The Second City), it was only a superficial similarity. Woody did and does write, memorize, rewrite and practice his jokes before delivering them. Much of his best stand-up material was recorded on Colpix records while he was still an active saloon performer. Although he doesn't like to do straight comedy routines anymore, if chance or necessity force him to perform, he will study the old records before he goes on.

When he did two or three shows a night in Greenwich Village, Woody was embarrassed to tell the same joke twice. But he has learned that audiences not only tolerate familiar material, they dote on it. It is the character of the Little Drip, and whoever his successor may finally turn out to be, that people come to see. They want him to look and say what they expect. If it's new material, fine, as long as it's in the Allen style. And if it's old material—even word for word—that's okay, too.

Of all Woody's comic routines, the famous "Moose" sequence has remained the most popular over the years. "I shot a moose, once," he tells the audience. "I was hunting in upstate New York, and I shot a moose. I strapped him onto the fender of my car. I'm driving home along the West Side Highway. But what I didn't realize was, the bullet did not penetrate the moose. It just creased his scalp, knocking him unconscious. In the Holland Tunnel the moose wakes up, so I'm driving with a live moose on my fender and the moose is signaling for a turn. And there's a law in New York State against driving with a conscious moose on your fender, Tuesdays, Thursdays, and Saturdays. And I'm very panicky. And then it hits me—some friends of mine are having a costume party. I'll go. I'll take the moose. I'll ditch him at the party. It won't be my responsibility. So I drive up to the party, and I knock on the door. The moose is next to me. My host comes to the door. I say, 'Hello, you know the Solomons.' We enter. The moose mingles. Did very well. Scored. Some guy was trying to sell him insurance for an hour and a half. Twelve o'clock comes, they give out the prizes for the best costume of the night. First prize goes to the Berkowitzes, a married couple dressed as a moose. The moose comes in second. The moose is furious. He and the Berkowitzes lock antlers in the living room. Now, I figure, here's my chance. I grab the moose, strap him to my fender, and shoot back to the woods. But, I've got the Berkowitzes. So I'm driving along with two Jewish people on my fender. And there's a law in New

York State, Tuesdays, Thursdays, and especially Saturday. The following morning, the Berkowitzes wake up in the woods in a moose suit. Mr. Berkowitz is shot, stuffed, and mounted at the New York Athletic Club. And the joke is on them, 'cause it's restricted."

This routine is a classic example of Woody's style as a cabaret comedian. First of all, the whole story is based on an increasingly surrealistic premise. Starting slowly, Woody convinces his listeners to accept an absurd situation, then piles on gags for twist after twist played off the original idea. To begin with, the idea of Woody Allen shooting a moose or even hunting in the woods is funny. In fact, the real Woody would never do such a thing. A totally urban man, Woody gets agoraphobia if he has to drive to the suburbs. The inevitable hilarity evoked by the moose routine—Allen has been using it essentially unchanged for nearly ten years—comes from its cumulative effect and the play on Woody's comic persona, rather from any single joke.

But the real groundwork of the moose joke, and all of Woody's best routines, is the funny and touching description of the outsider trying to get in. In this short little set piece (it takes Woody about two minutes to tell it) there are at least three sets of interlopers: Woody in the woods, the moose in the city, at the poor Berkowitzes anywhere at all. With each change of the outsider, we move up a level in accumulated absurdity. Here, as always, what the joke really lampoons is the comic personality of Woody Allen. He is the essential outsider whose outlandish and futile attempts to get in will always be good for laughs. Woody is really the only person mentioned in this story. He is the city boy who couldn't and wouldn't shoot a moose if the moose were trying to shoot him. He is the Jewish person who would have to be stuffed and mounted before he could get into the New York Athletic Club. But most of all, Woody is the moose. It is only a bit less absurd to think of Woody mingling at a party, scoring, being sold insurance, than it is to picture the moose. One always has the sense about Woody Allen that he sees himself as passing as a regular human being. He mingles quite well, really, but there's the nagging fear that somebody will discover that the moose suit doesn't come off.

Not that Woody's humor is consciously symbolic. He has said many times that he doesn't plan the personal threads that run through his jokes. He just tries to write material that seems funny. By this time, that statement looks a little disingenuous. Sixteen years of analysis and nearly as many as a public figure have given this comic a pretty good idea of what other people think of his personality. But much of his best comic writing, for movies and magazines as well as for the stage, has a quasi-spontaneous quality that indicates it comes out of his soul. Woody doesn't have to try to make all his characters represent himself, they just naturally do.

Allen's self-absorption is his strength as a humorist, and potentially his greatest weakness. It may yet turn out that Woody can't write any other kind of character than the one he has always played. Meanwhile, though, "The Moose Mingles" is a capsule history of Woody Allen's life.

Woody's strength has always been his material. His very personality was opposed to the mental and physical requirements of being a nightclub comic. The early success of his act was totally a response to the funniest material on the circuit. That could carry him. However, he was obviously concerned that much of his material never reached the audience simply because of his lack of theatrical expertise. But Woody could learn, he could change. He could and he would discover how to deliver the material so that people would realize it was funny. Eventually, of course, he discovered and perfected the Little Drip, the indispensable vehicle of his comic routines. But somewhere along the way, he learned diction and timing. Woody's humor was witty, intelligent, sneaky. The only way to get it across, he discovered, was to say it very slowly and distinctly. His delivery became almost a parody of an elocution lesson, with final consonants bitten off so hard that they caused static in the sound system. The pregnant pauses after one of his delayed-action punchlines were so long that you would start to suspect a stillbirth. And then the laugh would come, bigger because it was also laughter about how the lines could sneak up on you. "I want to tell you a terrific story about oral contraception," he would say. "I asked this girl to sleep with me, and she said 'no.' " Silence. Then rolling laughter. Applause.

Woody got good. He got very good. He played Chicago and San Francisco and Las Vegas, where he kept to his room. You were no more likely to find Woody at an after-hours table with Jack Carter and David Frye, talking shop and exchanging dirty jokes, than you would have been when he was at Midwood High. Then, as now, the only important thing to Woody was getting the laughs. After a while, he hung out with Sahl or Dick Cavett. But the gin mill scene or the dope scene or the Friar's Club scene were all anathema to him. He didn't and doesn't go to Hollywood parties, and he won't play the Academy Awards. Comics before Woody used booze jokes like bread and butter. Younger comics after him—David Steinberg, Robert Klein, Cheech and Chong—used reefer material the same way. Woody never has and never will use either. He is not now nor has he ever been part of any in-group. He is completely his own man.

Although his comedy grew up in saloons, Woody refused to acknowledge his setting. He had no squelchers for hecklers, doggedly delivering his jokes over whatever buzz or banter there was in the room. After he became big, when he knew the audiences were with him, he would sometimes take questions from the audience and develop something from them. But this was not so much a way to relate to the people as to bounce new material off them. Mort Sahl was one of the first comedians to whom the material was the primary thing. For Woody, it was the only thing.

Woody has said more than once that he and Bill Cosby are the last of the stand-up comics. What he means, of course, is that they are the last, so far, to start as cabaret comedians, make it big, and stay big. At first glance, the two would seem to have nothing in common. Cosby is a natural hipster. He has the understated confidence and grace of the athlete, which he is. And he has an unselfconscious feeling for other people that comes across the footlights as genuine warmth. Not a professional humanitarian like Dick Gregory, he is a humanitarian anyway, just by personality.

So how does Cosby resemble Mr. Nervous Twitch, the perennial misanthrope from Brooklyn? Only in this: each of them knows himself well, understands his own style and how to stick to it. Cosby is Woody's direct opposite, the one-man in-crowd. And Woody would never do ball game routines, even though he, too, was something of an athlete. Cosby stays largely away from "intellectual" material, though he has had much more classroom education than Allen has. Both men have a well-developed, highly individual style, and the very good sense to stay within the bounds of that style. Milton Berle and Henny Youngman could easily exchange their entire joke libraries and keep right on working. But nobody could do Cosby or Allen material except Cosby or Allen. Nobody who has come along after them on the nightclub circuit, including Cheech and Chong, has been so indispensible to his own material. Maybe that's why nobody who has come along after them has been able to hold the popular imagination so persistently.

Cosby and Allen got their start in the Village in the early sixties. It was a moment in American history when individual grace and style were more honored and rewarded than they have been since. John F. Kennedy was in the White House, and the country felt rich and young. Kennedy made it a point to remark, in his inaugural speech, that the reins of government had passed into the hands of people born in this century. That line got the biggest cheer of the day and must have embarrassed old General Ike, standing there in the cold. The civil rights movement was still gathering steam, and for once it was okay, even better than okay, to be Jewish, black, or young. A lot of people, especially those like Allen and Cosby, who had been part of the "silent generation," thought that having style and being true to your own identity could help clear up a lot of our country's problems.

If neither Cosby nor Allen had much to say in their acts about politics or the Kennedys or civil rights, they were as much a part of the times, as aware of what was in the air, as anyone. Neither was a topical comedian. They usually dealt with the deeper issues: growing up, being loved, doing something well (or badly), getting laid, getting old, and dying. But both men approached their work in exactly the way that was indicated by the Kennedy era, with style and vigor.

That the Kennedy era ended so prematurely was an accident, or a plot, of history. If Kennedy had lived, of course, the chunk of time bearing his name would have been much longer. There are those who say that if Kennedy had lived, the romance between him and the American people would have soured. It would have been revealed that he was a poor tactician, and perhaps a poor strategist, as well. But the things in Kennedy and his young wife that the country had fallen in love with were values it had been wanting for a long time. We had conquered our physical frontiers, and were ready to tackle the new frontiers of developing true civilization. Americans wanted to hold on to their historic respect for individualism, but to express it in a way that would work for the greatest social good. We loved the Kennedys for their grace, their wit, their willingness to be exactly who they were and not to apologize for any of it: not the Boston accents, not the new and suspicious fortune, not the Catholicism. We all wanted to do what they did—to be great and still be ourselves.

Mort Sahl and Bill Cosby and Woody Allen were like that, too. They looked natural to us, the same on stage and off. In contrast, it was pretty easy to imagine clean Henny Youngman loosening up a little offstage, just as it was pretty easy to believe that sweet-faced Mamie Eisenhower tippled in private. Whatever the truth was, the old style comics, and presidents for that matter, didn't have the trick of seeming to be spontaneous the way the new ones did. If Woody Allen said on the stage that he didn't drink, he probably didn't. (He doesn't, either.)

Of course, the most important subject that finally came out of the closet in the sixties was sex. After about a hundred years of skirts on the piano legs and a yawning gulf between nice girls and good girls, it all just spilled out into the light. Freud was fully accepted, if widely misunderstood. Sex was a real part of life. You got horny, naturally. What's more, women got horny too. What your mother sacrificed her youth to keep you from finding out was all over town, on the newstands, in the magazines, in your own family, when your daughter moved out of her room and into an apartment with her boyfriend.

In the thirty years before 1960, one of the big fringe benefits of the stand-up comedians' life, and there weren't too many benefits for beginners, was the sudden easiness of sex. There were showgirls, girls running away from little nothing towns, and just regular chippies. You came from a poor Jewish family in Brooklyn, where the only women you knew were always down on their knees washing the kitchen floor to get ready for the Sabbath. The only thing you knew about sex was that it was mighty hard to come by. You probably have to get married to get any, at least on a steady basis. But you found out you were funny and you got a few stand-up gigs, and then you went on the road, maybe to vaudeville theatres, maybe to little clubs, maybe in burlesque, as the human glue that held together a parade of strippers. And then, you got to screw. With bells on, if you wanted. It was still dirty, and you still didn't make many jokes about it in your act, but it was one of those in-group things, a major fact about your life that set you apart from the repressed and puritanical common people.

Then came the sixties. *Playboy* magazine. Beat poets. The sexual revolution. Teen-age sex all around you, like you would've been glad to cut off your leg for twenty years ago. Even the president probably fooled around some, and nobody much held it against him, as long as he was discreet. And here came Woody Allen, talking about sex in his act, not as something to be sniggered at and quickly glossed over, but as one of life's problems—how do I make it with girls? He may have been the first American comic to present an extended routine that actually takes place during intercourse and orgasm. And he was no Lenny Bruce; Woody never was and never could be considered a "dirty" comic. Some of his material made Redd Foxx look like a tame kitty, but he just didn't see the jokes, or sex itself, as essentially dirty. There was a problem. It was infinitely comical. But it wasn't obscene.

It must have galled a lot of the old comics,

and the old straights, too, to see young people having sex they'd never dreamed possible: up front, with no nastiness and very little guilt attached. It must have galled some of them even more to see Woody Allen get up and make money from jokes about this new license. When they got together in private, the old greats regaled each other with their filthiest material, the kind of stuff they could never come close to using onstage. They dropped their pants like high school boys, and never failed to crack each other up doing it. The idea of Allen, Cosby, or Mike Nichols, or even the young Dick Gregory hanging around some club getting plastered and making penis jokes is impossible to entertain. Just as it's impossible to imagine most of the new comedians doing hard drugs like Lenny Bruce.

The new reverence for Lenny Bruce, who was a grade-B comedian with a grade-Z lifestyle, and nasty besides, can only be explained in terms of the gathering speed with which everything changed after 1960. Bruce is seen as having literally died defending those things we all take to be commonplace now: the right to say "fuck" in a public place, for example, now widely supposed to be one of those inalienable rights with which the creator has endowed us. (In fact, Bruce died of a narcotic overdose, and narcotics are as illegal now as they ever have been.) What

Bruce was really hounded for—and nobody denies that he was hounded—was the same thing the peace movement was hounded for in the sixties, being uppity. Lenny really was guilty of what Woody Allen is often accused of: holding nothing sacred. He didn't even bother to take care of his own body and mind, much less lavishing love on his fellow *schmucks*. Another reason we like him, to our discredit, is that as a suicide we think of him as another in a line of popular heroes we imagine were just too sensitive to live. Janis Joplin, Jimi Hendrix, Marilyn Monroe, and Sylvia Plath are other victims of this posthumous lionization.

Woody, by contrast, wants to live. He thinks a lot about trying to cheat death and the futility of that attempt. If there is something just a little self-destructive about getting up in front of a bunch of strangers and making fun of yourself, Woody's comedy is ultimately a survivor's art. When he was a performer, he tried to make the material survive by perfecting it, using it over and over until he could deliver it just right, making the laughs a sure thing. When everything was as good as it could be, Woody cut records to make the laughs even more indelible. He has long since understood that to stay alive you have to change, and he drives himself, congenital cowardice notwithstanding, to do something at least a bit different every time he plans a piece of work. The need for permanence helps to explain Woody's moves into film and the printed page, though he was probably happy enough to quit throwing himself, a sparrow in a pack of hyenas, into the saloon life.

Lenny Bruce, despite the far-out reputation he eventually acquired, was one of the boys. Lots and lots of his "sick" and "degenerate" jokes were stolen from more conventional comics, like Buddy Hackett, Red Buttons, Phil Foster, Joey Adams. The only difference was that while the other guys told them offstage, Lenny used them in his act. In his early days, before Lenny bashed his head into hard drugs, he was just another Brooklyn Jewish crazy guy, working the Catskills resorts, doing nutty things with the other comedians in his spare time. Woody Allen has never run with any gang, and he never will. He never worked burlesque, never did *shtick*, never was a table man. During the days when he was maturing his act in the Village, Woody didn't know that he is really a writer rather than a comedian.

Nevertheless, Woody was enough like the true stand-up comic to make it, especially considering how much funnier he was than most of the others. He was at least a Brooklyn Jew, in a profession where fully 90 percent of the regulars are Brooklyn Jews. Dick Gregory and Bill Cosby and Godfrey Cambridge are, or were, the only true black one-liners. Bob Hope and Lord Buckley, Cheech and Chong, a few others are something besides nice Jewish boys from New York. Carol Burnett and Phillis Diller and Lily Tomlin aren't nice Jewish girls from Brooklyn, either, but women in comedy is a whole other story. Mostly, the traditional American comedian, the man with the head full of wisecracks and the belly full of some vague hurt is from a very specific background. He is the child of Middle- or Eastern-European immigrants, nearly always Jewish and nearly always poor. This particular wrinkle on the age-old theme of the jester is an American contribution to the world and a Jewish contribution to America.

In the sixties, when comics like Sahl and Berman and Bruce began to appear, critics wrote that the face of cabaret comedy was changing. Woody Allen was another who was often called the new breed of comedian. In truth, stand-up comedy was finished. The market simply wasn't there any more. Nobody went out to theaters or clubs, at least nobody much, to see some wise-acre shoot off his mouth. If it seemed for a moment that we were taking our fools more seriously, it was only the moment before we realized we didn't want fools in the old, simple-minded sense, at all. We don't want variety shows with a lot of gagsters and trampoline acts from Bulgaria. They don't amuse us any more. Americans in the seventies fell hard for television's kind of merry-making, the sitcom. Archie Bunker, yes; Uncle Miltie, no.

Among the so-called new breed of nightclub comic, only those who knew how to change survived, like Mel Brooks, or who were growing in a different direction all the time, like Woody and Bill Cosby. Mort Sahl, whose searing social satire seems to have started it all, declined into a one-issue man, hammering away at the Kennedy assassination and the Warren report until he stopped being funny and became a fanatic to his audiences. Shelly Berman, a master of routines about those tiny wrong things that gang up to spoil the big things, got a reputation for being a nitpicker, a difficult man to work with, a guy who went crazy, if you served drinks or collected change during his set. He began to lose jobs and never be asked for lots of others. Cosby went to television, Godfrey Cambridge to the movies, Dick Gregory to jail, and on the lecture circuit, and to jail. Bruce died, and new names with the old style—Robert Kelin, David Steinberg—seemed to come and go as in a revolving door. Berle, Hope, Georgie Jessel, and Henny Youngman began turning up at each other's testimonials more often than anywhere else. George Burns starred (after the death of Jack Benny, the original star) with Walter Matthau in a vaudeville nostalgia movie called *The Sunshine Boys*.

Las Vegas remains. It's a town full of show biz people in the old style and tourists who like them and like to gamble. Buddy Hackett, Johnny Carson, Sammy Davis, Jr., and Don Rickles still get big money for engagements in Vegas. The new comedians make records or movies or do Broadway reviews. Woody Allen's last regular turn as a classic comedian was in 1968, though he has made one tour since. There was no new material in his act, and, except in Vegas, his crowds were respectable, not huge. The Allen movies, on the other hand, drew increasingly large crowds, and there was lots of ticket money left over for the celluloid antics of Mel Brooks and company.

America has grown tired of that uniquely American creation, the cabaret smart-aleck. It seems that we want our funnymen to be both more sophisticated, more wise, and also more innocent. We want to see social significance, no matter how superficial, and we want context, no matter how surreal. We hark back with pleasure to the sweetness of early Marx Brothers, Charlie Chaplin, and especially Buster Keaton. Many of us are on the lookout for the kind of uncomplicated nuttiness in a long-ago song of Groucho's: "Show me a rose, and I'll show you a stag at bay. Show me a rose, or leave me alone."

As a people, we are on our way to discovering that misanthropy won't work. It won't get us what we want and need in this crowded world. The old greats were raised in an embattled society, spoon-fed on racial hatred, class hatred, national hatred, and self hatred. The new comedians seem to be looking for a way to be funny as an alternative to hate, rather than a way of expressing it. At their best, they aren't mocking themselves or their audience, but the whole human condition. Hey, look at us. Ain't we funny? Most of us are tired, finally, with putting ourselves down as ugly Americans, burning our cities, bashing heads, bombing Gooks. At least in our comedy, we are looking more and more toward something with a gentler sound. Richard Pryor we like, even those of us who aren't black, and Flip Wilson. We go for Archie Bunker, but we like Sanford and Son just as much. Character, situation, human relations.

If Woody Allen grew up in the old-time cabaret tradition, he has been fast enough on his feet to incorporate a lot of the new tradition as he grew. True, he still plays for the laughs, unable to believe that people will stay with him if he lets some time go by without gags. But he seems to be groping toward an understanding of character, and the old hostility is much less in evidence in his latest work, both cinematic and written. He shows every sign of having more capacity to grow and learn, and very likely his work will be around when nobody knows the difference between Lenny Bruce and Dustin Hoffman. For the most part, the cabarets are closed, and Woody Allen knows it.

3

Mr. New York

"Look. You should know this about me. I'm from New York. I have a *slight* metropolitan accent."

Why is the crowd already laughing? Because there's no place else on earth or in outer space that Woody could have happened. He's metropolitan through and through. Nobody's ever looked, but probably the bottoms of his feet are stamped "Made in New York." Everything is seen through a Fun-City lens.

"I wrote a science fiction story once. One day, at precisely four o'clock in the afternoon, everybody in the whole world falls asleep. Everywhere: Russia, China, the United States. They sleep for one hour. At five o'clock, we all wake up and discover, strangely enough, that everybody on earth is in the pants business. We're making cuffs, sewing seams, and cutting cloth, when a flying saucer lands. The people get out, and they're wearing shirts, ties, jackets . . . and no pants. And they say, 'Are the pants ready?' And we say, 'No, could you come back Tuesday?' And they say they have to have them, 'cause they're going to a wedding."

The New York mind.

New York City is a place that, more than once, has threatened to secede from New York State. Very likely, they'd like to secede from the Union, as well. They're a unique people, tough and funny. Workers. Wisecrackers. Ironic and mean and tender all at the same time. It's what you get when you cross Middle-European peasants with robber barons and let the mixture ferment. You get Barbra Streisand. You get Benny and Berle and Youngman and Sam Goldwin and Charlie Feldman and oh, just everybody. You get Woody Allen.

Privately, Woody will tell you he's not happy anyplace else.

"The woods make me nervous. All those damn birds in the morning. I can't sleep. Really. There's so much *noise* in the country."

When Woody talks about "the country," he means Beverly Hills. You couldn't get him to the real country if you bound and gagged him and threw him a freight car in the middle of the night. The idea of having to spend any substantial amount of time in places like Denver and Prague and Budapest—places considered by some to be great cities—makes him quiver.

His life has been lived on subways and sidewalks and candystore stools. It was subbasements and tough neighborhoods and tougher public schools. A little later, it was Times Square and press agents and small saloons. And big saloons. And television studios. And wood-panelled offices. Then it was hotels and commercial jets and trailers behind the stadium and after-hours clubs for playing and listening to jazz.

The places most people never get to see even once are the places Woody has spent his entire existence. And the people! Second-rate Catskill clowns. Hustlers. Shuckers. Jivers. The hip and the hangers-on. And in the other corner, you have the nervous Jewish parents. Don't eat that, it'll give you indigestion. Don't lie on the beach, you'll get sun stroke. Wear your rubbers. Keep your hand on your wallet. If anyone touches you, yell for a cop. It's another world.

Woody is as intensely urban as a man can be.

"I am at two with nature." Funny? Sure. Fact? Indubitably. To him, the countryside is interesting only as a shooting location. And not only nature. The whole physical world makes him nervous. Besides trees and the weather, the thing New Yorkers can't handle is technology. Mr. Urban Man is fighting on two fronts. There's the war with nature, and the war with machines. Guess who loses both?

If he gets in a few good licks on his television set, he gets in back, in spades, from a talking elevator.

Where else can you earn a living, where else can you just plain *live*, with no physical work whatever? Paris, maybe. London is big enough to foster the right frame of mind. But then, the British have their dogs and their country weekends. They wouldn't let it happen. That leaves you-know-where. In New York, you can live your whole life—working, playing, sleeping, socializing—without ever seeing an open space larger than the lobby at Rockefeller Center.

You can get every physical job done for you in the city, if you have enough money and ingenuity. In a funny way, New Yorkers are narrow. If you're a tailor, you have no idea how to plaster your own walls or repair your toaster. There are a lot of jobs for people who can only work with their heads, or maybe their mouths. Even poor people in New York buy cakes from the bakery and hire professional movers. In the rest of America, you do it yourself. In New York, you hire a specialist.

There's also no other city on earth where even the *goyim* are Jewish. In the whole country, Jews make up 1½, maybe 2 percent of the population. In New York, they are 30 percent. And if you're a New Yorker, even if you're not Jewish you're Jewish. Yiddish words and phrases are a part of the common language in New York, and there's nobody anywhere in the five boroughs who doesn't know what a bialy is. There is no place in the world today, including Tel Aviv, where a Jew of Eastern-European heritage would feel more at home than in New York. The culture that was European Judaism is gone, wiped out in a war that threatened to erase a whole people from the earth. The tradition is still remembered and celebrated only in New York.

Where else could Woody Allen have come from? Where else could he go? He has said many times that Flatbush was the heart of the Old World, and he makes no effort to hide that he is a child of that world. Although he is now primarily a film maker, there is no danger whatsoever that he will "go Hollywood," or even spend much time in California, if he can help it. Except for *Sleeper*, he has brought all his films back to New York to edit. His permanent residence, although he moves all the time, has been within the same twenty blocks on the Upper East Side ever since he started earning enough money to afford the rents.

Like most New Yorkers, Woody shows a touch of xenophobia. People in the city tend to believe that New York has the best and the most of everything, so why would you want to go anywhere else? *Don't Drink the Water*,

Woody's first play, shows some of this suspicion of foreigners and things foreign. The water, naturally, is the water in other countries, which Americans who traveled abroad were continually being warned against lest they develop some local disease, usually intestinal, that was indigenous in the native population. The story of the play concerns misadventures of a typical American sitcom family who accidently get mixed up in espionage during their European vacation. The play, produced by David Merrick, ran a year and a half on Broadway, and according to one critic, contained at least 500 laughs. This in spite of mixed reviews and many changes of cast and personnel along the way. In fact, *Water* was not just a hit, but an instant classic as well. Woody still receives regular royalty checks for the play, ten years after it was first produced. There is almost never a moment when some little theater group somewhere in the country isn't doing *Water*, which runs a good second to *Harvey* as the most popular vehicle for amateur acting companies.

When it opened in New York, *Water* starred Kay Medford and Lou Jacobi, with Tony Roberts. Woody was nowhere to be seen in the cast, nor did he direct it. This play was the first and only full-length work that Woody had something to do with—but not everything. He wanted very much to have a successful play, and he did. But the work, for all its popularity, is fairly anonymous, precisely because the Woody-character doesn't appear. At that point in his career, making it big on Broadway was more important to Woody than his distinctive style. His years of writing for other comedians had taught him how to get the most general, sure-fire laughs. In *Water*, he went after the laughs in a big way, using all the techniques of verbal humor and plain gag writing that he knew, which was pretty much all the techniques ever invented. And he won. He had his hit. Although it's safe to say that everything he's written since has been better, or anyway more interesting, nothing could top the pleasure his Brooklyn soul took in that first big city hit.

But once was not enough. Even though everyone has said for years that the New York theater is ailing, failing, or actually dead, Woody's affection for the invalid is boundless. It's clear that you don't get rich and famous writing or directing or acting in Broadway plays these days. Anyway, Woody is already rich and famous from his movies. His motivation to go on writing for the legitimate theater must come partly from a love of the form, and partly from being Mr. New York.

A recent newspaper survey showed that most respondents in an upper-middle-class

Brooklyn neighborhood said that when they went out, they went to the theater. This is in contrast to the entertainment habits of most Americans, which center around movies and bowling. In other words, New Yorkers still love the theater. In fact, the price of a hit show on Broadway has become so ridiculously high that few people can afford to go regularly. But city folks are still proud of their theater— really the only dramtic center in the nation— even if they never go.

The next Woody Allen play to hit Broadway was *Play It Again, Sam*, featuring Woody, along with Tony Roberts again, and Diane Keaton for the first time. If *Water* had been a hit, *Sam* was a knockout, illustrating the truism that if Woody's work is good without him, it's always better with him. Or rather, it's better if he writes it with himself in mind. Woody has not yet written a play that, like his movies, could only be acted by him. But the idea behind *Sam*, the little nervous guy who's trying to be Bogart with the women, is so much more interesting and personal than the idea of *Don't Drink the Water*. Once Woody is able to relate a character to his own personality, the character rounds out. Otherwise, there's no person there, only a comic foil. In the London version of the play, Woody's part was taken by Dudley Moore, from *Beyond the Fringe*. Many people felt that Moore played the part better than Woody. But then, Woody is not exactly an actor. If a role suits him, he looks well in it. If not, he's at a loss. Woody stays the same, so if improvement is wanted, it must be in the part.

Woody's part in *Sam* is Allan Felix, a neurotic movie reviewer and, once again, a flop with chicks. Felix is obviously meant to be confused with Woody Allen, and he was. Because of the popularity of the movie version, Allan Felix is still Woody's best-known role, the one most people on the street identify him with. Why "Felix?" It may have been meant as an ironic comment on the Little Drip, since felix means happy, and Allen is seldom that. More likely, Felix was meant to suggest a cat, probably a pussycat. If it hadn't been for a *Pussycat*, after all, Allen would never have been in a position to trot his neuroses out on the stage.

One of the good things about doing plays is that it gives Woody a chance to play to live audiences, and to goof. Making a movie is like putting together a scrapbook—you glue, evaluate, unstick it and glue it again. Especially with Woody, film making is a rather solemn, perfectionist project. But in the theater, the show must go on. When lines are blown or a piece of scenery collapses, actors are forced to use their wits to hold the play together and move it along. This gives a training in spontaneity that Woody needs more than most actors. Another appeal the theater has for Woody is the challenge it offers the illusionist. Movies are so obviously mechanical, the smallest effect is supported by banks of lights, cables, sound systems, and assistants hovering just out of camera range. The stage offers the chance for actors, directors, and writers to make something out of nothing. Great theatrics are those that can breathe the illusion of life into the rigid, classical form of a bare platform with a curtain.

Since childhood, Woody has been an illusionist, a magician. In his cabaret act, he managed to, as he says, "give the illusion of three dimensions" to a comic character that became familiar to millions. In spite of his lack of feeling for improvisation and his strong need for orderly pre-planning, he loves a put-on. In New York, the put-on is more common than the practical joke. People are much more likely to kid you in this verbal way, spinning out an elaborate tale with very little relation to the truth, than they are to shake your hand with joy buzzers or put squirting devices under the seats of their toilets. Over the years, Woody has become a master of the public put-on, especially with the press. His earliest interviews are usually very straight, and one senses Woody trying earnestly to communicate the truth about himself and his comedy. After a while, though, he recognized that readers and reporters would much rather have him be funny than truthful, offstage as well as on. So he started writing jokes and routines for himself to do during interviews.

By now, Woody has developed the put-on interview into a new and subtle art form. Unlike in his act or his movies, the jokes here are subtle and disguised. He wants to fool the reporter, to be taken seriously and reported straight. Usually, he is. Once in a while he will get too broad, as he did in *Rolling Stone*, and it will be evident to everyone that it's all a shuck. Usually, though, he's amusingly successful. There are no belly laughs in this kind of comedy, sometimes you're not even sure where the joke starts and stops. This put-on of the press is the closest Woody has come yet to the in-group comedy of the new comedians. There is still a certain hostility, of course. There always is, when you're trying to hoodwink someone.

"Woody Allen craves chocolate malts and is verrry fussy about how they're made."

"Woody Allen fills his apartment and says he wants a Monet, if he only had the Money."

"Woody Allen walks to work."

"He rides to work in a limousine."

"He hates his ex-wives."

"His best friends are his ex-wives."

No wonder Woody gets sick of reporters trailing after him, writing down every *hem* and *haw* that drops from his lips. He is a very private man. He knows, as all New Yorkers know, that you have to watch your fences like a guard dog. Otherwise, somebody's bound to slip in through one of the holes.

For years, Woody has been slipping outlandish little lies into his interviews. Francine du Plessix Gray asked him if he thought he was more obsessed with death than the average man.

"Oh, definitely, definitely. A lot more. I mean, death doesn't sound like fun, right? There isn't a nice thing you can say about it." The minor-league put-on.

Sometimes, it's more elaborate. He goes to a restaurant with a reporter, somehow without a jacket. He must wear an ill-fitting restaurant jacket. Score one. The jacket's too big and hangs over his hands at the cuffs. The Little Drip. There's no way to prove he did it on purpose, of course. But he's not an absent-minded man, and if there's anything he knows about, it's comic effect. He leans across the table and tells the writer that the only sport he's good at is ping-pong. Yeah, right? A medium put-on.

His real name is Heywood. (No, it isn't).

His real name is Yitzak.

He gets all his ideas from a "colored gentleman" who lives in his closet. "Every American has one."

His father works as his doorman. (No actual verification on this one, true or false. The doorman won't talk.)

He writes his movie scripts all at once, in one night. (Really? says the reporter. Really. Deadpan.)

This business of what Woody's real name is has given a lot of writers trouble over the years. Maybe Woody got the idea from *Grimm's Fairy Tales*. Wherever the inspiration is from, he comes back to it over and over. He told reporter Alfred Bester that the only thing he won't reveal for publication is that super hush-hush name. Bester understood. He would not mention the name.

A major-league put on. By the time of that interview, Woody's real name had been mentioned in every single other interview he'd ever granted. It was part of absolutely every other piece, long or short, ever written about the tricky Mr. Konigsberg. He explained to poor Bester with all the seriousness of a religious practical joker that he had spent his whole professional life building up a reputation as Woody Allen.

"I don't want the public to be confused, you know, by knowing my real name. It might hurt what I've worked for." Was there a catch in his throat? Did his voice break, just a little? It isn't recorded.

He offered to tell Bester the name (Rumplestiltskin?) in confidence, thus making the writer possessor of a secret that had been in the public domain for ten years. It never did Cary Grant's image harm for the public to know that his mother named him Archie Leach. If Leach couldn't touch Grant, what harm could Konigsberg do to the famous Woody Allen? Who can remember Konigsberg for more than five minutes, anyhow? In New York, even ordinary people have a sense of the media breathing down their necks. How much more oppressive it must be for a public figure. How delicious it must be to put one over on the press once in a while. Woody scores.

One of the questions reporters never fail to ask Woody is whether all his years of Freudian analysis have changed him. "It's dull," he says. "In, whine for fifty minutes, out." He likes Freud, though, and his approving statements about the Viennese doctor's pessimism seem to be genuine. Like every stand-up comic, and like most New Yorkers, Woody is a pessimist, too. As he says, "People are *not* dynamite." You can hardly live in Manhattan, where a thief is born every minute, and feel that human beings are the greatest thing that ever happened to the earth. To a real city man like Woody, however, people are the only thing. In contrast to Emerson or Thoreau, modern, urban man draws next to no inspiration from ponds and trees and the ancient, rock-ribbed hills. Cityman gets his ideas from other people, from books, and from inside his own head. Whether or not we're sociable, we are necessarily social. Woody does admit that psychoanalysis has broadened his outlook, given him a larger appeal. Cityman needs help in relating to his fellow humans; much more than Countryman did. After all, in Emerson's day, they didn't press in on one quite so much. What Emerson would have though if he'd lived in a Park Avenue apartment like Woody Allen, there's no way to tell.

Perhaps if he'd been a twentieth-century New Yorker, Emerson would have had a shrink, too. More New Yorkers do than any other group anywhere, including Los Angeles. Woody once said that when he was in Europe, he participated in a "neurotic exchange program." He saw a European analyst for six months, which meant that a European boy could see Woody's analyst in New York. Good for a few laughs, but the fact is that Freud has never caught on on his native continent the way he has here. Nor has it ever been as commonplace for folks in Florida or Ohio to undertake long years of therapy. To the rest of the country and the world, psychoanalysis is still something exotic. That fact may explain why Woody has been able to mine that vein for laughs over the whole extent of his career. It may also help to explain why he can't leave New York. Where else could he find an analyst who'd understand him?

Once, trying to explain why analysis had not been the answer to all his problems, Woody said, "It's like when you have your clarinet repaired. When you get it home and play it it sounds good, but not as good as you had hoped." Woody should know. He's been playing the clarinet since childhood, and, as with everything he does, he's been getting slowly and steadily better. The clarinet is an instrument made to order for Woody's personality: precise, low-key, absolutely unresponsive to the powerhouse treatment you can give the piano or the trumpet. At its best, jazz clarinet has a singing, wailing quality that is just like Woody—both brail and solid. The clarinet, like other woodwinds, is a matter of precision and delicacy. It makes onamental music, like the flute. Lots of little trills and runs, and heaven help you if you like to really pound it out. As Pauline Kael has observed, you can't goof around with the clarinet. Woody doesn't. He plays traditional, New

Orleans style jazz, not Dixieland, but an authentic reproduction of the real thing, Jelly Roll Morton and early Armstrong. He is scrupulous and very careful in his arrangements, as in everything else. He has his own band, or, as he is careful to say, he is a part of an ensemble, though he is by far the most famous person in it. For a while, the group, the New Orleans Funeral and Ragtime Orchestra, played regularly at a pub in Manhattan. They can also be heard on the sound track of *Sleeper,* along with the Preservation Hall Jazz Band, an authentic New Orleans group whose youngest member is in his sixties.

Woody has huge admiration for the greats of classic jazz. He once said that if he could live his life over again he'd like to play ball until he was too old, and then play music. But though he is very good within the narrow confines of melodic, rhythmic New Orleans jazz, Woody has no understanding of or interest in improvisational jazz, especially not of the deeply expressive and personal sort played by black musicians since Dizzy Gillespie.

Certain classical musicians—Joshua Rifkin, William Bolcom, Itzak Perlman—have recently made popular recordings of classic ragtime compositions written by undervalued black American composers like Scott Joplin and James Scott. Like them, Woody is an interpreter in music rather than an innovator. His strength as a clarinetist is that he can reproduce the authentic original sound. For *Sleeper*, he went to New Orleans to sit in with the Preservation Hall Band. According to all reports, he behaved very much as a junior admirer should, not telling the band what to play or how to play it.

In the North, even more than in the South, blacks have what the whites, despite superior wealth and position, cannot have. Black people are hip. Staying hip is a full-time occupation, and only the very young or the unemployed really have the time it takes. Certainly Woody Allen doesn't have the time, nor does he have any natural talent that way. But, like most city kids, he has the desire. Lots of urban white kids today affect a black style, do-wopping and hanging out. Woody never had the time for that, either, pushed from behind as he was to hurry to open a drugstore and claim his key to the bourgeoisie. Not being a WASP with a silver spoon in his mouth, he wanted success, if not exactly on his mother's terms, more than he wanted to be cool. But playing New Orleans jazz is his own orderly way of paying tribute to what is most spontaneous and creative in American music, that is, black music. The truth is, American music *is* black music. We have never produced any other really original native forms. The musician in Woody Allen acknowledges it, and then keeps quiet.

Verbal though he is, Woody Allen is basically a quiet man, whose life takes place inside his head. It is a tribute to his persistence and discipline, rather than to natural talent, that he can play jazz or tennis or do the kind of physical clowning he did in *Sleeper*. This characteristic explains more than any other why Woody is a city boy, and why he'll stay a city boy. Where else but in the city, particularly in New York, are you so completely free to live in your mind? In New York, you can arrange your life so you don't have to cook, clean, sew, garden, build anything, repair anything, or move anything. You can live in an elevator building with air conditioning and steam heat, so you don't even have to walk up and down stairs or open windows. You can take a subway or a cab, or if you're rich, like Woody Allen, you can hire drivers. That way, you not only don't have to walk anywhere, you don't have to bother with maintaining a car, either. You can hire a housekeeper and a cook, and if you're hungry in the middle of the night, you can order take-out pizza or Chinese food. For the well-heeled, who are usually the ones who know how to live by their wits, the city means services. In Beverly Hills, even the movie stars have to worry about keeping the lawn cut and getting the Rolls tuned up. They don't have to do it, but they have to give it some thought. In New York, one can avoid such mind-idling.

The city also means a kind of association that is perfectly suited to the loner. When you live in a small town, people are always dropping by to sit in your kitchen and chat. If you want to see people, you get together. In a small town, folks live in each other's laps. But in New York, you can go out onto the street and be with people without making any social commitment. Stand on the corner of Third Avenue or Lexington for a while, or wander through Bloomingdale's, as Woody likes to do, and you know for sure that you're part of a society. For those who need more warmth from people, the lonely crowd is very unsatisfying. But for city types like Woody Allen, its all the satisfaction they need or want. For some, knowing people means being intimate with their souls. For others, and Woody is one of these, it just means knowing that people are out there.

Like all artists whose subject is mostly themselves, Woody continues to draw heavily on his personal past. That past is his Brooklyn Jewish background, and it fills his work, giving his writing its characteristic rhythm, as well as many of its jokes. He has always been aware of the comic contrast between the Yiddish-tinged coloquial speech of New York and the larger subjects that concern mankind. An early joke was about the feelings of inferiority he had vis-à-vis a talking elevator. "I have a *slight* New York accent, but the elevator spoke very well." Later, he would use the New York intonation as a comic contrast to flights of purple prose: "Discotheques are fun because even the dreariest of women look wild when they're doing those things to that beat and their hair falls around and their hips swing and their eyes roll back. What's not to like?"

When he first started in nightclubs, Woody used to put himself down by saying he looked like a farmer. "I was conspicuous because I'd just had a seafood lunch, and I'd forgotten to remove the bib. I looked like a farmer." During the sixties, it became quite fashionable to look like a farmer. If Jacqueline Onassis didn't show up in Big Mac overalls, her children did, for sure. And the young people who made up Woody's biggest body of fans wore nothing but jeans, day and night. People in droves were denouncing the city and leaving to start communal farms in Maine.

In Woody's city aesthetic, it will always be best to look like a dude. Walt Frazier wouldn't turn up anywhere in overalls. For Woody, his habitual garb of jeans, sweaters, and saddle shoes is a clown costume. On him, it's funny. But for most of the rest of his generation, or maybe the generation just after, depending on how many years you figure between generations, jeans and sweaters are what you mean when you say clothes. So Woody toned down his remarks about farmers. He stopped wearing his sharp, city-boy suits, and his face lost its smart-ass look. But this is artifice. Underneath, he is, as he was, a wisecracking Brooklyn street kid who doesn't want to be mistaken for a bumpkin.

In New York, where he is instantly recognized as he steps out of his door, there's not much chance of being mistaken for anyone or anything else. To cut down recognition, he usually wears a battered rain hat, pulled low over the tops of his glasses. Still, you don't notice him rushing to the south of France or even out to Easthampton to be alone. It's better to have taxi drivers yelling, "Hey, Woody!" at you than to be a nobody. It's better to have to fight for your privacy, as most celebrities do, than to have to fight to be known. It's pleasant, once in a while, to be sitting in the Russian Tea Room and have some lady come up and ask you to autograph her napkin, "For my daughter."

Woody's friends, a small, tight group, are all New Yorkers, either born or transplanted. There's Louise Lasser, of course, and Diane

Keaton. And there's Mickey Rose, a boyhood pal who collaborated with Woody on *Take the Money and Run* and *Bananas*, and Marshall Brickman, a guy who can write like Woody Allen almost as well as Woody Allen can, and who worked with him on the scripts for *Sex* and *Sleeper*. There's Tony Roberts, the actor, who has appeared in two Allen films and a play, and there's Dick Cavett, a friend from the early cabaret days when both were comedy writers trying to get jobs under their own names.

If there is ever a movie version of "The Woody Allen Story," Cavett is a natural choice for the actor to play Woody. Although he is a Nebraska boy, and still retains the twang, Cavett looks enough like Woody to be his brother. They speak alike, accents aside, and have the same cultivated but self-deprecating style. But mostly they think alike. They are more witty and more subtle than most comedians before them. Both have been repeatedly accused of being intellectual, even *too* intellectual. But they are not intellectual, and each of them has said so. They are intelligent. There's a difference. Woody and Dick Cavett have both demonstrated by their persistent success and popularity that America is ready for intelligence in humor. We are too sophisticated now for pratfalls and mother-in-law jokes. Radio and television have educated us. Floor wax and stomach remedies are being sold to us, not by slick ladies dressed like Betty Furness, but by women who, if they're not Jewish mothers, could certainly pass. The urban, literate clown is an idea whose time has come, and whose name is Woody Allen.

As a matter of fact, one of those ladies whose New York voice and unglamorous face has sold a lot of drain cleaner and curry powder is Louise Lasser, Woody's friend and second wife. She is a winning comedienne in her own right, with a style just that you'd expect from a woman who learned it all from Woody. Friends for years before their marriage, Woody and Louise split up about the time that *Play it Again, Sam* opened on Broadway.

The plot of *Sam*, about a guy whose wife is divorcing him and who can't seem to relax with the other women friends keep introducing him to, is closely parallel to what was happening in Woody and Louise's lives when he wrote the play. To further confuse life and art, it was Diane Keaton, both on stage and in real life, who became the new woman in Woody's life. In a group like Woody's, though, a little divorce and change of partners isn't enough to break up the old gang. Louise Lasser remains one of Woody's best friends. She played parts as his wife and as the female spider (later cut) in *Everything You Always*

Wanted to Know About Sex, after she was divorced from Woody.

There's no end to the jokes New York generates for Woody. He'll even put in references that nobody *except* New Yorkers will understand, if he thinks they're funny enough. In *Sleeper*, Woody is told by a man of the future that the world of the seventies began to degenerate when "power was seized by a man named Albert Shanker." In New York, audiences screamed with laughter. The rest of America frowned in puzzled incomprehension. (Shanker, a controversial figure, is the head of the teacher's union in New York.)

Woody doesn't care. He thinks it's a mistake to eliminate material just because it's regional.

"In Europe, they laughed harder than anywhere at the scenes in *Bananas* where I'm being threatened by tough guys in the subway. I thought they wouldn't go for it, because it's New York stuff, but they loved it. After that, I left the New York stuff in."

One of Allen's all time favorite routines was about his encounter with New York muggers. "I was always being sadistically beaten about the head and neck." So he moved into a doormanned building. "Very safe and secure. Two weeks later, I'm attacked by my doorman." They liked that line just as much in

L.A. as they did on the upper East Side. Better. New York is the town the rest of the world loves to hate.

Woody's idea of playing God is to wear blue suits and take taxis. God is a New Yorker. "I'd tip big, because He would have. I got into a fight with a guy, and I forgave him. It's true. Some guy hit my fender the other day, and I said unto him, 'Be fruitful, and multiply.' But not in those words."

WOODY ALLEN,
alias Allen Konigsberg, a/k/a The funniest man alive today.

THE GREAT WOODY ALLEN TRIVIA TEST

Woody Allen has an image, probably the most visual and consistent image of any contemporary personality. Everybody knows that face. On these pages you can test yourself on your knowledge of Woody, his career, and his films. Answers are on a page at the back of the book.

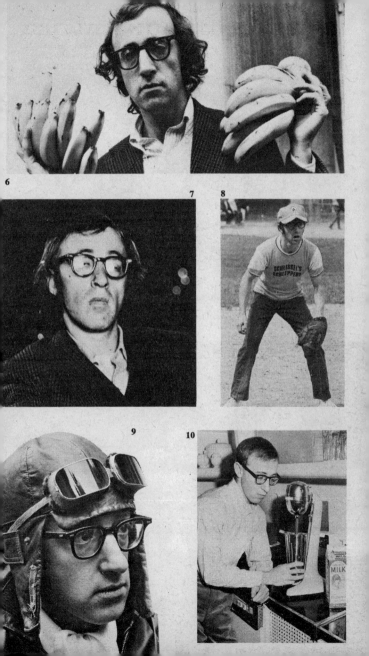

11

12

13 14

15

17

18

19

20

21

22　**23**

24

25

26

27   **28**

29

30

31

32

33

34

35 36

4

He Found It at the Movies

He's perfect for the movies. Anyone could have seen it. He's funny-looking, for one thing. A rubber face like we haven't seen since Jerry Lewis.

"I paint things in broad strokes," he says. "I make faces. I go for the big laughs."

What else were our comic movies ever made of? Come to think of it, that kind of comedy goes back before movies. Before vaudeville, even. Woody's a classic, like the little goon who tagged along with the snake oil salesman. They'd roll into town and stop a while at your local gaudy Blue Mouse or Roxy Theatre to sell you doped-up patent medicine and laughter.

These days, comedy comes not via circus train but by underground cable and the wide silver screen. With both Woody and Mel Brooks packing them in all over town, it looks like comedy might just rescue the movie industry. Movies should never have left comedy in the first place. No heavy Swedish drama has ever been a better flick than Buster Keaton or the Keystone Cops.

Woody grew up in the movie palaces of Flatbush Avenue. Most of his generation are ex-movie freaks. We've been longing, without really knowing it, for a few good movies. Like the old days. Light, fast, funny. The kind of thing that just won't come across on the endlessly yattering tube. We want what we used to take for granted on all those Friday nights and Saturday afternoons in the dark. Woody is giving us back the nutty, mile-a-minute movie. He makes them for an audience of teen-agers, sitting down in front and digging it, just the way Woody used to dig Dr. Kildare or Laurel and Hardy.

In truth, the audience drawn by Woody's cinematic comedy is far wider than that. And spreading. They are teeny-boppers, sure. But there are also young marrieds, college kids, businessmen, musicians, nurses, and cab drivers. Up to now, the audiences have been mostly white and middle class, but that's changing, too. People who would have liked Chaplin are starting to like Woody; maybe even some who were Chaplin's contemporaries, and haven't seen a good movie since. People who read *Vogue* are lining up to see his films, not to mention people who read *The New Yorker*. Critics like Pauline Kael think

Woody Allen has a good shot at universal acceptance, or as close to universal as you can get in the crazy-quilt fabric of American society.

The movies, in short, seem to be Woody Allen's natural home. During the four years he worked regularly as a stand-up comic, Woody's material never changed. He changed, growing more confident as a performer, a public personality, but the jokes stayed the same. But once he hit the movies, the shape of Woody Allen's comedy began to grow like a Walt Disney beanstalk. Each new Allen movie represents a seven-league jump in his understanding of the medium and of his own comic potential.

Woody got his start in comedy as a word man. Words are the stock-in-trade of all the saloon comedians, who very seldom relied on clownish props. No squeegie dolls or light-up noses or inflatable shoes at the Stardust Lounge. In his first months as a stand-up performer, Woody's looks were as straight as they could be. It never occurred to Woody or his managers to change the way he dressed. Visual comedy, except for mugging and maybe a stiff-kneed walk, was never part of the cabaret scene. It's true that Milton Berle was forever climbing in and out of baggy pants and flowered dresses, but that was only later, after he became Mr. Television.

But for Woody, interest in the visual aspects of comedy came along early. Even before he made his first movie, he was at work on the Little Drip, his facial expressions, his posture, his old jeans and saddle shoes. He began to dress up his jokes with mugging and shrugging to squeeze even more laughs out of the assertion that he was "a stud." A lot of the nervous mannerisms, like leaning on the microphone for support, were kept in Woody's act long after he'd got over his stage fright. His saloon act, while still in the cabaret style, began to take on a flavor of mime, the much older tradition of the nonverbal clown.

By 1964 Woody Allen was a big-time comedian, playing rooms like Mr. Kelly's and the Blue Angel in New York. It had taken him two years since he first stepped onstage at the Duplex, mouth dry and voice breaking from sheer terror. He still intends to be a playwright, but fame and fortune were never conditions he disdained, and it seemed he was well along the way to both in his role as a nightclub comic. Enter Charles K. Feldman, a big, well-dressed man, who sits quietly at his ringside table, not guffawing, but just appreciating.

Feldman was a Hollywood producer of the old style, the kind who could grab Woody Allen by his corduroy lapels and snarl, "Boy, stick with me. I can make you a star."

Feldman sat at the Blue Angel, watching and listening, for one night, maybe two. And when his producer's intuition told him he'd seen and heard enough, he offered Woody the job of scriptwriter on his next movie, to be called, *What's New, Pussycat?*. As Woody told it later, he was on stage, when "in walks a Mr. Feldman, a producer, and he just adored me, on sight. He thought I was attractive, and sensual, and good-looking—just made for motion pictures." Pause. "He's a little short man, with red hair and glasses."

In spite of the jokes, Woody did not enjoy the six months he spent in Europe, working on *Pussycat*. In one way, it was a new world for him, lavish and lazy. The entire cast moved to Rome for six weeks, gave each other dinner parties every night and saw the sights every day. Money was never an object with Feldman—he knew how to make it and he knew how to spend it. Then the word would come that filming was not going to be in Rome after all, but in Paris, and the whole cast would pack up and move to Paris. It was not a life Woody Allen had any experience with, and it made him nervous. For a man who can happily eat steamed fish and vegetables every night for a year, expensive dinners on the Via Veneto don't hold much charm.

And if Charles Feldman was loose with money, he was stingy with power. Woody found himself back in the same kind of working conditions he'd suffered on "The Garry Moore Show" and countless other stints writing for big-name comedians. He was the writer, but he had no control over his own material. Nobody had ultimate control over a Feldman picture, except Feldman. He and Woody fought about everything: where the film would be shot, who would star, down to Woody's script itself, line by line. The cast, which was supposed to have been headed by Warren Beatty, was finally headed by Peter O'Toole and Peter Sellers. Woody would have preferred himself and Groucho Marx.

Of course, Woody was right, in a way. *Pussycat* would have been infinitely funnier if Woody had starred as the habitual womanizer who wants to settle down, but somehow just can't keep beautiful girls from turning up in his bed, even parachuting into his convertible. And imagine the wacky psychiatrist as played by Groucho. He's supposed to be helping the ladies' man to confine himself to one woman, but what he really wants is to get his hands on just one or two of the silky young things who keep falling into his patient's lap. If the movie has been done Woody's way, it would probably be a small comic classic by now, like one of Buster Keaton's first films. But it might never have become what it did under Feldman's management, namely the biggest money-maker of any comic film, ever. It was this fact, not Woody's script, which was tampered with until it was unrecognizable, and not his small part as Victor Shakopolis, that won him freedom in Hollywood to do his next movie the way he wanted. Movies are a big business, and the one thing big business always respects is big profit.

Woody's association with *Pussycat*, painful as it was for him at the time, moved him into a position of instant power in Hollywood. Studios and producers had decided he was a winner, a creative type, a genius, and they were willing to give him millions of dollars to create. *Pussycat*, a gaudy, disjointed piece of flim-flam, was somehow just the right flick for 1965. It had lots of beautiful women: Capucine, Romy Schneider, Ursula Andress. It had blue-eyed Peter O'Toole for a romantic lead, and wild-eyed Peter Sellers as a comic foil. Sellers was in the process of losing the tight, witty comic style he had acquired on the *Goon Shows* with Spike Milligan, but his disintegration into slapstick seemed just the right thing in *Pussycat*. Finally, the film had enough gorgeous sets and gorgeous clothes and gorgeous technicolor to tickle the eyeballs of the younger generation, who were busy discovering psychedelic drugs, day-glo paint, and the Beatles. The total gross earnings of the movie were over $17 million.

When the movie finally opened, in June of 1965, it was roundly panned by the critics, a drubbing it deserved. There were a few things that everybody liked though, both the critics and the thousands of moviegoers who rushed to make Charlie Feldman rich. One of them was the title song, written by a little-known young composer named Burt Bacharach. Another was Woody. Somehow, nobody blamed him for the ham-fisted script, which one reviewer described as "neurotic and unwholesome." His association in the public mind with a phenomenally popular, jet-setty movie did him nothing but good. He got a lot of mileage out of it in his act, which he kept doing for two and a half more years, and he took care to say offstage, but on the record, that his script had been radically altered by the producers.

Ten years later, of all those associated with *Pussycat*, only Woody seemed still to be a rising star. The women, of course, are not as young as they were, and since being beautiful and sexy was their whole act, they are less called on of late. Peter O'Toole is more likely to be playing character parts than romantic leads, and Sellers seems to have wasted himself, though he still retains his incredible skill at voices and disguise. Charles Feldman died in 1968. Of all of them, Woody probably derived the most benefit from *Pussycat*. Even at the time, he got more publicity than almost anyone else. O'Toole and Sellers were already famous, and Feldman was already rich and powerful. But Woody was a complete unknown in movie circles before 1965. After, as if by accident, he was a force to be reckoned with. *Pussycat* had given him a taste of the international movie crowd—enough to tell him that, like alcohol, his body wouldn't tolerate it. It gave Woody and his agents enough film contacts to last a lifetime, especially after its enormous financial success.

What his association with Feldman and company didn't give Woody was confidence. Feldman himself was the sort of benevolent dictator who insidiously undermines the egos of his protegés by altering and replacing everything they do. Although he had now written and acted in a major motion picture, which gave him a large amount of pull on the Hollywood purse strings, Woody was not yet ready to strike out on his own. Working under the shadow of Charlie Feldman, he had not really had a chance to study the workings of film-making or to evaluate what he could do as an actor. So many of his scenes were cut in favor of more Sellers or more O'Toole that, although he wrote himself a large part, in the finished film his role was rather small. It was clear to Woody that he could write and star in comic movies—he knew how much better *Pussycat* could have been—but he needed more experience.

The chance to polish his acting skills came with an offer to play, ridiculously enough, James Bond's nephew. The vehicle, *Casino Royale*, was disappointing to Woody fans and to 007 fans, but working on the film gave Woody the chance he needed to learn the mechanics of movie making. Working on *Pussycat* was a nauseating round of duck dinners, script changes, and fights with the boss. Woody, in fact, had left the company halfway through the shooting, saying that Charlie Feldman was free to remove Heywood Allen's name from the credits. But *Casino Royale*, while also produced by Feldman, was a straight acting job, or rather, a nonacting job, since Woody was free to create and play the character he always played, the Little Drip. Although he received no writing credits for *Casino*, his nephew role showed all the attributes of his stage persona, and in fact, marked the beginning of the visual Woody, successor to the mantle of Buster Keaton and the immortal *Charleau*.

But not in that order. And not right away. On his way to full-fledged directorhood, Woody invented a new form, the falsely dubbed comic melodrama. This is a rough description of *What's Up, Tiger Lily?* A work that proved, if nothing else, that Woody had learned something about successful titles from Charles Feldman. The concept was preposterous: Japanese drama with *non sequitur* dubbing, mostly ad-libbed, by Woody and assorted crazies. It's unclear now whether this bit of xenophobic juvenalia was Woody's idea or was dreamed up by someone at American International pictures, but whichever, it was the first of the "Woody Allen movies," and has its place in the archives. The final product, with the Japanese footage chopped up and refitted with improvised nonsense, made back its price and then some. In Hollywood, that's good enough.

It was enough to induce Palomar studios to put up more than $1½ million for Woody to write, direct, and star in *Take the Money and Run*. This picture displayed the Little Drip, now clearly derived from Chaplin, in his most fully realized form. Basically, the Drip had always been a character out of the movies, a living fiction posing as a suitable replacement for Benny and Berle. Woody used to say that he used special lighting behind him on big dates, "to give me the illusion of three dimensions." As long as he was playing nightclubs, there was something so accurate about the idea that sometimes audiences failed to respond to it as a joke. But once the Drip climbed up there onto the screen, you saw him almost as an archetype: the born loser, fictionalized completely, and therefore more completely real.

In *Take the Money and Run*, Woody plays Virgil Starkwell, a bungling desperado who is an extension of the earlier stand-up routines about his having wanted to be an arch-criminal as a child, before he discovered he was too short. Virgil also marks the apex of the baroque period of Woody Allen's names. (If there was ever a classical period, all records have been lost.) In live performances, Woody used to tell jokes about cronies named Eggs Benedict and Guy de Maupassant Rabbinowitz. ("So I said to him, 'take your hands off her, Guy de.'") Victor Shakopolis, from *Pussycat*, was a more restrained and more descriptive name for the Drip: Victor, as in victory, and Shakopolis, which might be either shack up city or shaking city. Woody used this one again, for the fellow in *Everything You Ever Wanted to Know About Sex* who attempts to scare the giant breast back into its bra with the help of an exorcist's cross.

Virgil Starkwell probably got his first name from the contrast, which Woody still finds amusing, between classical references and his own frail person. Starkwell was probably based on the unlikely exploits of Charles Starkweather, who, with his teen-aged girl-friend, terrorized and shot a string of people across the American South in the late fifties. (*Badlands*, made fifteen years later, was a serious treatment, in movie-fiction form, of the same incident.) Whatever his derivation, Virgil is a boyish, red-haired bankrobber, so inept that when he presents the bank teller with a hold-up note, she can't read it.

"What does this say," asks the teller, reading the note as if it were an overdraft notice.

"It says, 'please put fifty thousand dollars into this bag and act natural. I am pointing a gun at you.'"

"That looks like *gub*. That doesn't look like *gun*."

Eventually, of course, Starkwell is caught and returned to prison with a sentence of eight hundred years. Still, he tells an interviewer, he has no regrets about his life of crime. "I think crime definitely pays, you know, the hours are good, you're your own boss, and you travel a lot..." Virgil, obviously, will never learn, even if he lives eight hundred years.

Take the Money was pretty much a sure thing for Woody, because it featured the same kind of verbal Little Drip comedy that had gotten the laughs in nightclubs. His costume was the same as in his latter days as a saloon comic—sweater, hornrims, scared rabbit face. He had not yet assumed the angelic look of the idiot savant that stamps his character in

Sleeper. Nor had he discovered the *coup de grace* of the saddle shoes. There were some good visual bits in *Take the Money,* including two robbers in Groucho masks, complete with eyebrows. But the conception is that of a word man, a parodist, in fact, rather than a visual artist. *Take the Money* represents the first and last appearance on film of the fully realized Drip. Virgil Starkwell is a pureblood loser, without much of the zaniness Woody is capable of at his most relaxed.

Making *What's Up, Tiger Lily?* was a lark for Woody. Always uncomfortable with his physical self, he was completely at ease here in the role of unseen dubber. Though the movie is usually dismissed as silly, it contains some classic Allen lines, such as this description of the unfortunate Japanese bad guys, "They kill, they maim, and not only that, they call information for numbers they could easily look up themselves." The whole business had a screwy, Jonathan Winters kind of spontaneity that wouldn't surface again in Woody's work until *Bananas.* It certainly was not in evidence in *Take the Money,* which is as controlled and stylized as anything he has written for the *New Yorker.* In his second film, Woody was starting to feel successful as a film maker, a director even, and he was beginning to protect his flanks. The longest-running guaranteed laugh milker in his bag of tricks was the Little Drip, the pathetic clot whose looserhood is his whole personality. He was to discover that the Drip played less well in the movies than he did on the cabaret stage.

Not that *Take the Money* was badly received. On the contrary, it turned out to be the work that made Woody's reputation as a director. By the time *Money* was released, the public knew him as a scriptwriter, actor, comedian, playwright (*Don't Drink the Water* and *Play It Again, Sam*), and more. Like all Allen films, this one made money, and played to good, if not super critical approval.

Most important, the movie convinced Hollywood moneymen that Woody's way with audiences was no flash in the pan. Even after *Tiger Lily*, Woody found it hard to get a studio to commit $1.6 million to him as a director-star. But after *Money*, he was suddenly golden. United Artists offered him two million as a budget for his next film, plus a three-film contract. More important even than the money was the almost unheard-of artistic freedom UA gave Allen. After initial approval of the story, United Artists would have no veto power over Woody's judgment, whether the issue was script, casting, shooting, or final cuts. In fact, UA had bought themselves a good deal. Woody is as meticulous a worker on his movies as he is when he writes. He usually finishes his pictures on time and within budget, also unheard-of in Hollywood. So far, only *Sleeper* has been over budget, and even at three million, a Woody Allen movie is cheap compared to *The Godfather* or *Love Story.*

Most critics agree that *Bananas,* Woody's first film for United Artists, is his funniest to date. This is not to say that it was the most consistent or most cinematic or tightly plotted. In fact, it is none of these. Like *Tiger Lily, Bananas* is wildly uneven, alternating high hilarity with relatively dead patches. Visually, it is such an improvement over his earlier movies that one can hardly believe the short time between them.

As he has shown over and over, he is nothing if not a quick study. In a society where adults seem to learn nothing and children nothing much, we are astonished to see a public personality who grows and learns and changes before our very eyes. By the time he made *Bananas,* Woody had grasped the visual techniques to translate his verbal humor into real cinema. True, he was not perfect at using these new tools, sometimes he dropped them altogether. But the high points in *Bananas* are equal to any comic moment in any film ever made. One of the funniest of these, almost untranslatable into words, is the scene where Woody and the South American revolutionary band, having run out of food, decide to order sandwiches from the local jungle deli. The idea itself is amusing, but the sight of hundreds of green paper lunch bags, lined up on the counter of what could be a luncheonette from the corner of St. Mark's Place and Second Avenue, evokes instant hilarity.

Other bits in *Bananas* are direct translation into visual form of Woody's earlier cabaret humor. Early in the film, Woody, starring as Fielding Mellish, is molested by hoods in the New York subway. He had been playing this scene out verbally for years in his stand-up act. "I'm on the subway with my clarinet," he would say, somehow squeezing a laugh out of this reference to the instrument he plays, "and twelve guys come running through the subway car, but really hairy knuckle types, you know. Apparently they had just come from the settlement house, because they were dribbling a social worker." The scene in *Bananas* is simply the visual realization of his old routine, but it achieves a universality that no nightclub act could ever have. According to Woody, audiences in Stockholm, most of whom presumably were unfamiliar with New York, laughed as hard at that scene as did audiences in Brooklyn.

Bananas marks the first tentative appearance of what Pauline Kael calls Woody's "closet potency." Before this film, the Allen humor dwelt almost exclusively on his nebbishness. We forgot, and Woody encouraged us to forget, that his was actually a success story. At a time in life when most boys, from Brooklyn or not, were wondering what they could do in life, Woody was already a professional comedy writer. Before he was twenty-one, he was a celebrity, chased by reporters and entrepreneurs. In truth, he was what most of us want to be but are afraid to aspire to be: rich, famous, and good.

While Woody himself seems to have believed that his appeal was based on his weakness, what we really liked about him was the almost subliminal impression of strength. We didn't like him because we felt superior, or at least not only that. We liked him because we felt superior in some ways, and yet we could see how successful, how witty, how indirectly triumphant he could be. In spite of his foibles, which we laugh at, we secretly root for him. We want him to win because we sense that if he can, we can. People who don't understand this, and they include Woody himself at times, have said that audiences laugh at him because notion of his success—with women or adventure or technology—is so ridiculous. In fact, just the opposite is true.

Woody's character in *Bananas* is still a nebbish, or rather, a Mellish, but not such an all-out loser as Victor Shakopolis or Virgil Starkwell. Here, the classical epithet (Fielding probably means "strong") is not so forced, not so obviously played for laughs. Even though Fielding can't seem to sustain a relationship with the Girl (played by his second wife, Louise Lasser) or become a surgeon, he does, in his daffy Brooklyn way, become a revolutionary leader. The lowest spots in *Bananas* come when Woody declines to play on his strengths, as when he fails to seduce the beautiful lady revolutionary.

The plot of *Bananas* is like a series of dream sequences, connected mainly by the identity of the dreamer, Fielding-Woody. This looseness makes for a certain incoherence, a fault Woody displayed before in *Pussycat* and *Tiger Lily*. But it also allows him to rise on a momentary comic wind with a kind of spontaneity that was precluded by the careful structure of *Take the Money and Run*.

All of Woody's work, from his first days in nightclubs, has suffered from the unresolved contrast between tight control, which is the method most natural to him, and the demands of high comedy, which should at least seem to be unconscious and instinctive. Unlike Jonathan Winters, Woody is not an authentic wild man. He is a writer, a punster, a man of modest and solitary pleasures. Naturally, his attempt to make himself into a high-flying movie clown by sheer effort and intelligence has occasioned certain belly flops. But his success so far, which is considerable, encourages and amuses us.

After *Bananas*, Woody starred in a movie version of his play, a hit on Broadway, called *Play It Again, Sam*. (The title was based on the dialogue between Humphrey Bogart and the pianist, Sam, in *Casablanca*. Woody is well aware that the line was never spoken in the Bogart movie, but by now the myth is widespread enough to elicit instant recognition. In terms of structure, *Sam* is at the opposite end of the spectrum from *Bananas*. The plot is traditional and coherent, being the story of a neurotic writer, played by Woody in both play and movie, who is being divorced by his wife and having no success with other women. This, too, is an old theme from the cabaret years. One of his earliest routines concerned Woody's attempts, all failures, to find a woman to commit adultery with. "The Ten Commandments say you can't and the State of New York says you have to," he would say, referring to the blue-nosed New York divorce laws of the time. Unable to make it even with a trollop (she refused to believe that he still attended NYU, so he couldn't get a student discount), Woody finally let his wife commit the adultery. "She always was more mechanically inclined, anyhow," he would sigh.

Play It Again, Sam is the logical dramatic

extension of that vintage Allen routine. The difference here is that Woody does score, with his best friend's wife (Diane Keaton). *Sam* also marks the introduction of the first in a long line of elaborate theatrical tricks in Woody's work. Here, the gimmick is the ghost of Humphrey Bogart, who follows Woody to advise him on how to conquer women. This bit of hocus-pocus, done on stage with openings in the backdrop and elaborate lighting, was accomplished straightforwardly in the movie by double-exposing the film. As a child, Woody had loved magic tricks and sleight-of-hand, often practicing it by the hour. As a mature artist, he fell deeply in love with the comic possibilities of elaborate props and special effects. The movies before *Sam* are much more simple than what came after. Having learned what special effects can do, Woody has since tried to push them even more in each succeeding film.

But the shade of Bogart was gimmick enough for *Sam*. The mainstay of the play, which has proved enduringly popular, was the Walter Mitty-like fantasy of the awkward but lustful little wimp suddenly beneficiary of all the know-how of the legendary Bogie. The wimp, of course, was Woody. But *Sam*, of all Woody's movies, depends most on theme. It is a thoroughly *written* piece, and the Woody part can be played just as well, maybe even better, by other actors. It is a well-wrought play, smooth and completely un-goofy. The real roots of *Sam* are not in hero-worship of Bogart, whom hero-worshipping Woody has never named among his idols, but in his early intense admiration for playwright George S. Kaufman. This was exactly what Woody had in mind when he decided to perform his own material in clubs to support himself while he wrote plays. (An earlier play, *Don't Drink the Water*, was also a Broadway hit, but was never filmed.)

The smooth, seamless construction of *Sam* excludes the high comic moments that occur in *Bananas*, but it also excludes the awkward lows. Audiences loved it, both in play and movie form. Woody had his picture on the cover of *Life* magazine, and they asked him to write the article inside, as well. The movie made him a real star, and his face began to be recognized on the streets. The gross income on the picture so far has been over $11 million, more than the earnings of his other pictures combined. Still, it is far from his funniest work, and was thoroughly criticized for being far less than he was capable of.

Although he says he is insensitive to criticism, either negative or positive, Woody was certainly touched by the blows *Sam* received. Pauline Kael, perhaps Woody's greatest fan among critics, and surely the most articulate and thoughtful one, detested *Play It Again, Sam*. And even as it was being filmed, Woody was trying to publicly separate himself from it, telling reporters that he was through with such glossy and superficial treatments. It must have been a disappointment for him to have fulfilled his childhood dream of becoming the urbane, well-heeled playwright and be told that the result was not his best work. But his greatest strength had always been his ability to learn from his mistakes and plunge ahead. His next cinematic offering would be *Everything You Always Wanted to Know About Sex—But Were Afraid to Ask*, a title purchased from Dr. David Reuben, who had already ridden it to fortune and notoriety.

Sex, proclaimed in advance by Woody to be "far out," was another string of self-contained fantasy sequences, and made even less attempt at sustained plotting than *Bananas*. Whether it was in reaction to the criticism of *Sam*'s slickness, or just Woody's way of flexing his alternate muscles, his scenario for *Sex* was a kind of free association on the theme of sex jokes. It includes the battle between Woody and the mammoth breast, as well as a love affair between Gene Wilder and a sheep, Lou Jacobi as a transvestite, spread seductively on a silk bedcover in nothing but his black bra and garter (and his five o'clock shadow), and Woody and a cast of thousands as sperm, waiting to be shot off on their mission of conception. The original footage also contained a scene between Woody and Louise Lasser, dressed in costumes that must have been made out of brown shag carpeting, impersonating the mating act of Black Widow spiders. "This gives you some idea of how much fun these little creatures have," Woody said at the time, "and why they always look so tired."

The props and sets for *Sex* were obviously an enormous problem, and Woody was careful to find the best designer available, settling on Dale Hennesy, who had won an Academy Award for the sets of *Fantastic Voyage.* Woody's ideas were no less demanding than the challenge of reproducing in gigantic scale the inside of a human body. By the time he was ready to direct *Sex*, Woody was also ready to push the cinematic form, to define new limits for what could be done in movies. Until *Play It Again, Sam,* which was directed by Herbert Ross rather than Woody, Allen films had been downright ugly. As a director, he had cared nothing for questions of camera angles, lighting, composition. Working on *Sam* taught him how many things could be said visually that were not just translations of the verbal, but statements in their own right. *Sex* shows that Woody had learned that if the conception of a motion picture is verbal-intellectual, its execution is fundamentally visual-physical.

Because he is not a visual comedian, a clown, but rather a humorist, Woody was somewhat tentative about making himself the comic vehicle in *Sex*. For the first time he wrote scenes, such as Wilder's, in which he didn't appear at all. This, as much as the experimental nature of the form and its episodic structure, makes *Sex* vary widely in funniness. Like *Bananas, Sex* is consciously out of control, as if a master draftsman had purposely allowed the pen to slip in hope of getting more dramatic effects. There is no other way for Woody to approximate improvisation except to relax the tightness that is his normal condition.

But if he saw himself as unspontaneous, he mistook his ability, at that point anyway, to write for or about any other characters except Victor-Virgil-Fielding-Woody. The scenes without Woody in them were always a let-down, no matter how well played by others. As funny as Gene Wilder is, amply demonstrated by his work in Mel Brooks' movies, Woody and a sheep might have been funnier. As his projects became more ambitious and more elaborate, Woody increasingly felt the need for other actors, other characters. But his comedy had always been the comedy of self-preoccupation. His only joke, in essence, was himself. When he had managed, as in *Play it Again, Sam*, to write a part that could be played by someone else, he did it at the cost of losing that "surrealistic" tone that makes him Woody, and makes him truly funny.

In a Woody Allen film, much as in a Woody Allen monologue, the dramatic tension comes from conflict within the Woody-character. Even the women, who are often his personal friends, are flat. Woody believes, or says in public, that Louise Lasser and Diane Keaton are fine actresses and comediennes. If so, their work in Woody's films has never given them a chance to show it. And aside from "the girl," there is nobody in any Allen film who is even in the running for the Fully Developed Character Award. It is evident, however, from his written work in *The New Yorker* and elsewhere, that Woody is aware of this defect and is working on it. Given his demonstrated capacity to learn new tricks, it's probably only a matter of time until he can develop people as well as parodies and situations.

One important thing that Woody discovered in making *Sex* is the comic value of carefully realized visual fantasies. The burden of this discovery, of course, fell on set designer Hennesy, who deserved an award for his willingness to serve the shifting Allen imagination. Woody was not and is not, used to conceiving of jokes in visual terms. Often he needs to see a set or a location or a prop before he can decide if it will work. This means more time and more money, more overtime for the crew, more reworking and rebuilding.

The results are usually worth it. The giant breast sequence in sex is remarkably powerful, going through humor and into a sort of psychedelic giddiness. The idea of a huge, detached tit, is funny enough. But to actually see it, looming against a Kodachrome-blue sky in a cow pasture, is a mind-blowing experience. Woody has always been fascinated by breasts, of course. It's never been a secret. On stage he used to say that his childhood unhappiness was because he had been, "breast fed—from falsies." His taste in women runs to the well-endowed. One of the few things his friends can recall about his first wife is that she was large-breasted. But if, as his remarks and the breast scene would indicate, Woody is haunted by the female breast (the word "fixation" is better left to the shrinks), he has turned the obsession to advantage. At the preposterous moment when the breast, which Woody is attempting to drive back into its bra, shoots milk at him in an act of pure hostility, there is nothing left to do but laugh. If you thought you knew what it meant to be breast fed from falsies, you had no idea until that moment.

The most surrealistic segments in *Sex* function in an exact visual analog of the way his verbal humor works. As in the story of the mingling moose, you are induced to accept utterly fantastic situations by the clarity of the detail in which they are presented. The breast is truly moving in its verisimilitude. This must be the way a breast looks to a newborn baby.

In the sperm scene, Woody discovered a visual device that will serve him well in the future. Since we know him and his comic persona, we find it funny just to see a room full of men, all dressed in identical costumes, with one (guess who) in big, black glasses. *Sex*, in short, is Woody's first cinematic movie; the first to make use of the purely visual as aspects of his comedy. Like all the best of Woody Allen, *Sex* totters on the border between hilarity and plain bad taste, though whenever it topples over onto the tasteless side, it becomes dull. But when it is right, it's so right that you think the dreams you're seeing are your own, and you're surprised and pleased by their wit.

Sleeper, on the other hand, has no tasteless spots, no dull spots. It represents a return to control for Woody, newly competent as a film director. Although not tightly plotted like

Sam, Sleeper has a coherence and direction that are largely absent in *Bananas*, and completely absent in *Sex*. Woody has obviously left off worshiping Chaplin for a while, and taken up the idolization of Buster Keaton. His character, Miles Monroe, is newly restrained and somehow saintly, even down to his name. The dreamy look is very becoming to Woody, making him less harsh and putting·more distance between him and the old-style humor that he learned from the cabaret comedians. Fittingly, Miles Monroe is a time traveler, frozen in the twentieth century and thawed into dehumanized future by dissident doctors. Hence the title, one of Woody's best, though not a description of the film, which was an overground money-maker from the start.

But if *Sleeper* has no lows, it has very few highs, either. It displays Woody's enormous competence, but not his brain-zapped inspiration. Considering that it's Woody, *Sleeper* is almost in good taste. It shows a preoccupation with interiors and fancy shots that is new and not altogether welcome in his movies. He wants to tone down, to be less broad and goofy, but the effect is, predictably, a muting of the hilarity. The outstanding exception is the scene where the newly melted Miles, disoriented and not quite awake, is obliged to pose as one of the doctors to fool the police. Plunked into a wheelchair because he can't yet stand, Woody discovers that the thing is motorized, and proceeds to buzz up and down the room like a demented Lionel Barrymore, while the other doctors try frantically to make excuses for him. Unfortunately, this inspired improvisation comes at the beginning of the film, and is never equaled by the classic slapstick that follows.

James Thurber once said, paraphrasing Wordsworth, that comedy is emotional chaos recollected in tranquility. This is especially appropriate in the case of Woody Allen, whose natural orderliness continually threatens to capture and blunt his moments of sparkling lunacy. Many comedians, even great ones like Jonathan Winters, could use a little more tranquility. Woody could use a little more chaos. There is no doubt that he is suspicious of his emotional, out-of-control side. All of us are. But we long to see Woody give in, fly in the direction that the winds of lust and ambition carry him, and win by doing it. We would like it to be so for ourselves. But since we are ordinary people and Woody is one of our celebrities, we'll be satisfied if it comes true for him.

We are most on Woody's side when he plays the individual, recognizable as such even in the densest crowd of his peers. He doesn't belong, and never will, and this appeals to the part of us that feels the same everlasting alienation. Aside from the absurdity of it, which makes it funny, the sperm scene in *Sex* has that instant recognition factor that we associate with Woody Allen. Simply by keeping his glasses on and pulling a lock of red fuzz down over his forehead, Woody makes himself conspicuous and jarring in that roomful of white. On an abstract level, this is what appeals to us in the scene. Our eyes sweep down the white faces over white suits against white walls, looking for something to rest on. Then we find it, and it's Woody, and we laugh with recognition and relief. And all this excludes the fact that we are asked to believe, and do believe, that we're seeing a squadron of sperm, lined up like paratroopers in a bomber, waiting to be ejaculated into the upper reaches of some lady's reproductive tract. How could we not laugh? Even Norman Mailer must have laughed.

The robot scene in *Sleeper* has many things in common with the sperm scene. Most of all, Woody has carried over the automatic comedy to be gleaned from having the Woody-character stand out from a group, even when they're all dressed alike. In this case, since all the robots wear masks, Woody must be dressed a little differently to show up. The effect is achieved by having him in white face instead of a mask, and he retains, of course, his glasses. This is even funnier than the sperm scene, possibly because here he is overtly an imposter—a live man trying to pass as a mechanical one. The moment when we recognize him, his new, sweet, comic face shining through the white makeup, is one of the funniest and most memorable in the film.

The ending of *Sleeper*, like the ending of all Woody's movies, is remarkably unmemorable. The story just trails off and stops, very much as if Woody were winding up his cabaret act. Goodnight, folks.

What happens, in case you've forgot, is that "the girl," called Luna, decides at the last minute that she'd rather have Woody than the revolutionary leader. This is the converse of the way it worked out in *Bananas*, and a significant change for the Woody-character, who is no longer the Little Drip. But because *Sleeper*, consistent as it is, really has no plot, there is no particular point to the ending, and we forget it. Since the picture was going nowhere, had no point except to do yet another ritual dance around the body of our hero, there is no problem to be resolved by an ending. In Woody's more episodic pictures, this trailing off hasn't mattered so much. In *Sleeper*, for the first time, you feel the lack. Given the way Woody has worked before, the unsatisfied feeling has no doubt touched him, too, and we might expect to see the first strongly plotted Allen movie as his next work.

Love and Death is Woody's latest hit. A film that has both critics and movie goers waxing ecstatic. Without doubt, it is his finest film. This is Woody's big work; as *War & Peace* was Tolstoy's and *Crime and Punishment* was Dostoevsky's. The comparison is no accident. *Love and Death* makes fun of the big nineteenth century Russian novel, as well as of romantic love, revolution, war, and philosophy. Again Woody shares the honors with Diane Keaton, who plays Sonja to Woody's Boris.

The "love" in the title is the grand passion between Sonja, a sort of spaced out Natasha, and Boris, a duped revolutionary, who gets the death penalty. Boris Grushenko's approach to the death penalty: "Every man has to go sometime... but I'm different. I have to go at 6A.M. It was 5A.M. but I have a good lawyer."

Sonja is somewhat inclined to spread the love around, and she is even more inclined to talk philosophy when the moment calls for passionate surrender. Boris is the best incarnation to date of the Woody Allen character: eager, tentative, wobbling on the edge of failing to make it all come together.

As for "death," he is a businesslike character in a white sheet who goes around tidying up. Boris first meets death at the age of twelve. His only question is, "Are there any girls?"

Besides being a showcase for his matured

humor—more like the *New Yorker* than the Village Gate—*Love and Death* displays almost everything Woody Allen has learned in the film business. It used to be well known that Allen films looked like hell. This one is beautiful. It's a pleasure to look at, even in a purely technical way. Woody has come into his own as a director. From the costumes to the chosen locations in Hungary and France, everything works. Woody used to believe that "art shots"—subdued colors, the texture and framing of Bergman—wouldn't work for comedy. In this film he's made it all work.

Now that Woody's taken care of sex and death (more or less), those who know him confidently expect his next to be a wrapup on the subject of God. He has said of *Love and Death*, "This is the film God tried to stop." But if God goes to the movies, he'll see that he could do worse than Woody for an unauthorized biographer.

5

How to Write Like
Woody Allen

How to write like Woody Allen. Lots of people are doing it. Woody has become one of the most imitated writers around. He doesn't seem to mind, probably because imitation is the sincerest form of flattery, but mostly because he still does it better than anyone else. Lots better. Just the same, try your hand. Everyone loves a clown. Marshall Brickman does it. Of course, Marshall Brickman is an old friend of Woody's, and a collaborator on two of the films. Mickey Rose does it. Same story there. But if you don't happen to be one of the old boys from Midwood High, you can still give it a whirl. There are only a few thousand more or less simple rules.

1) Know your vaudeville. If you're too young to remember the real thing, see all the movies you can. Check out old Marx Brothers flicks, Bob Hope "Road" pictures, and the George Burns monologues from the TV series he did with Gracie Allen. Don't forget Laurel and

Hardy, Abbot and Costello. Steep yourself in routines like this:

"Hey, Joe, is that a new wig you're wearing?"

"Yeah, it is. How do you like it?"

"Terrific! Nobody'd ever know you're wearing a wig."

Develop intimate familiarity with words like "intro," "outro," and "Give him the hook!" There will be a pop quiz at the end of this chapter.

2) Cultivate free-floating hostility. Before you go to sleep at night think a lot about "killing them with laughter," and "knocking 'em dead." Go out of your way to listen to Don Rickles, Jackie Leonard, Jackie Gleason, Milton Berle. You don't have to be willing to sell your mother for a laugh, but it might be a good idea to tell Grandma to keep her bags packed.

3) Have a funny face. If you don't have one, get one. Raise your eyebrows up into your hairline whenever anybody is looking, and pull down the corners of your mouth. Let your wispy red hair grow down around your neck like a cheap wig. Better yet, get a cheap wig. Even if you never appear in public, these tactics will get you into the Woody Allen frame of mind and greatly improve your writing.

4) Work like the devil. Stock a little, stuffy

room with a typewriter (which you'll never use), pencil and paper, uncomfortable chairs, and a long rug on which to pace. Practice muttering to yourself in a barely audible voice whenever you're alone. After a while, do it even when you're not alone. Refuse all invitations for country weekends or anything else that smacks of "relaxation." If anyone tries to get you to go backpacking, say something obscene.

5) Refuse to pander to in-groups. Never make dope jokes, or any other jokes that imply it's us against them. It's not. It's you against everyone. Take a look at Nichols and May, Second City, *Beyond the Fringe*, and Firesign Theatre, but don't imitate them. They are all soft on good will. They have a bias. If you want to write like Woody, you have only one bias. Namely, you will make fun of anything that has a name. No favoritism in the Allen school of hard-edged comedy.

6) To cover your tracks, wear pullover sweaters and old jeans. Wear them all the time, but especially when you write. This will make you seem a little bit modern to those segments of your audience who are interested in that. A laugh, after all, is a laugh. You want all you can get, from any quarter.

7) Make fun of yourself. This is a major point. When you're writing for the *New Yorker* or the *New Republic*, you can lampoon things

like existentialism and the Jewish novel. When you're writing for the movies or the stage, stick to making yourself look ridiculous. This doesn't mean that you have to avoid making other people look ridiculous, however. Make grotesque faces at pretty girls when you go out, to give yourself practice. When writing, pick on your parents and any other close relatives. Make fun of all public institutions, such as higher education and the presidency, but be careful not to harp on any one thing too much, or you'll end up like Mort Sahl and Shelly Berman. Learn from other comedians' mistakes. But mostly, humiliate yourself. This will get laughs, and it will also help you feed your free-floating hostility.

8) Pay attention to words. Make lots of puns and jokes that turn on the literal meaning of expressions. Like this: "The only frigid woman I ever knew, I met her at a party, and I remember saying something witty to her, like, 'Let's you and me do it.' She said, 'Over my dead body,' and that's the way it always was." In vaudeville, this is known as the old switcheroo. Pretend you don't know that. Pretend you invented the idea.

9) Mention dwarfs all the time. Slip in a reference to a dwarf just when it is least expected. Dwarfs are intrinsically funny, as Walt Disney knew. Critics will say you do this because you are so short. Don't worry if you

happen to be tall. This kind of picky detail never makes any difference to critics.

10) If you do perform any of your material as a stand-up comic, be absolutely sure your audience gets every joke. You do this by leaving long pauses after every punch line. Wait until they laugh. If they never laugh, insult them subtly by turning around and talking to the wall. In print, the pregnant pause is accomplished by using a lot of periods. And very short sentences. And a new paragraph every two or three sentences. Also, keep your written pieces very short, to give readers a lot of time after they've finished to sit back and get all the jokes.

11) Hurt. You have to hurt. As Phil Proctor said, the traditional American comic is a man in pain. What's so funny about hurting? *Ah.* If you don't know, you're never going to write like Woody Allen.

12) Be sure you get across the message that the whole world is out to get you, even machines. Say things like, "I have a tape recorder. When I talk into it, it says, 'I know, I know.' " Avoid euphoric goofing or other indications that you're feeling good. You're *not* feeling good. Or, if you are, you shouldn't be.

13) Stammer. When you're writing scripts, write the stammers in, so nobody will forget them. Use devices like "*uh*," and "*umm*," and

dot, dot, dot (...). You don't improvise. You aren't spontaneous. You just give the impression of being spontaneous. You have to work very hard to create this illusion. See number four.

14) Pretend you don't understand what's funny about what you've said or written. Say things like this when you are interviewed: "I don't know why people find me funny, why they laugh at me. My reactions to everyday situations seem normal to me, but completely hilarious to everyone else, and most of the time I can't figure out why." If anybody suspects you're putting them on, open up your eyes a little wider and pull down the corners of your mouth a bit more. Jam your hands in your pockets and scuffle your feet. They fall for it, every time.

15) Stretch for the far-out connection. This is the most important one of all. If you want to, forget all the other rules, and concentrate on this one. It will get you called names like, "absurdist," and "surrealistic." There's never any harm in having a few four-syllable words associated with your work. Most important, it will get the laughs. Think up things like movie sequences where a giant, disembodied tit is chasing you through a field. Or cast yourself in the role of a pseudo-surgeon about to operate on a man who is nothing but a nose.

Use routines like this: "There is no question that there is an unseen world. The problem is, how far is it from mid-town, and how late is it open?" Or this: "I was not a good dresser, a short while ago. You don't wear argyle with dark blue. I'd wear dark blue socks and an argyle suit." Begin a joke in the standard, vaudeville way (see number one), then reach for a far-out punchline. To wit: "I asked the girl if she could bring a sister for me. She did. Sister Maria Teresa. It was a very slow evening. We discussed the New Testament. We agreed that He was very well adjusted for an only child." See how it works? The far-fetched connection. It must *be* a connection, but only of the most fragile and unexpected kind. Practice on your friends by saying the most bizarre things you can think of in casual conversation. Mention dwarfs and under-shorts. When they start crossing the street when they see you coming, you've got it. It helps to know something about Freud and Salvador Dali, but don't, for God's sake, take them seriously. Remember the laugh.

Learn to crank it out as though there were three of you. (It's perfectly okay if there *are* three of you, by the way, as long as each of you is less than one and a half feet tall.) Write all the time, and use whatever happens to you, no matter how personal and embarrassing, in your writing. In fact, since one of your objects is to humiliate yourself, the more personal and embarrassing it is, the better. When all else fails, assume your best basset hound look and tell people that you're a stud. If they still won't laugh, tickle them until they're unconscious and then claim it was because of your jokes. Passersby will be too busy calling an ambulance to dispute you.

It takes lots of energy to write like Woody Allen. You have to jazz, jingle, jitterbug, and jump. Woody writes like a roomful of snakes. He's active. He's nervous. He paces and ponders and pounds the desk. He cackles like a maniac when he gets a good line, racing over to the typewriter to put it down. He imagines a roomful of people, beside themselves with laughter. It's no wonder that Woody weighs only 115 pounds, soaking wet. He jitters off more pounds in his writing room than ten women in the sweatboxes at Jack La Lanne.

What do you need to do a Woody Allen imitation? Anything that gets a laugh, baby, anything at all. Fill up your author's cubicle with jester's hats and whoopee cushions and squeaking dolls. Don't forget the W. C. Fields posters and a long-playing album of The Best of Ernie Kovacs. His mind is a joker's bag of tricks, bottomless, motley, jangling. If you *really* want to write like Woody Allen, you have to get inside his head. It's crowded in there, cobwebby, confused. But look what that Pandora's box of a brain can produce.

In forty years, Woody's done it all, and then some. He's had a Henny Youngman phase, a Bob Hope phase, a Mort Sahl phase. He's done George S. Kaufman and Bogart and Chaplin and Keaton and Groucho. And he's only forty. There's no telling where he may go from here. Wherever it is, he'll be way out in front of all the others. That's the reason why he won't mind my telling you how to write like he does. He did it first, and he can still do it better. By the time you get where he is, Woody will have been there and gone.

But don't despair. There's room for more. And once upon a time, Woody had to learn it all, too. He was probably younger than you are when he started. Most Americans can't even read yet at the age when Woody first became a professional gag writer. But still, it's not in his genes. He wasn't born with a joy buzzer in his hand. If you have the drive, if you have the energy, if you have the pure, single-minded desire, and if you follow the instructions with care, you can write like witty Woody. If not, you can join the rest of us in being his fans. See you at the movies.

6

The Written Wisdom
of Witty Woody

The Man dropped out of two colleges in the same space of time it takes most freshmen to memorize the campus map. It was ridiculous for him to have gone to college in the first place. Still, it always bothered him that he had no degree.

"My first wife was a philosophy student, you know. She used to get me into these long arguments where she'd prove I didn't exist."

So Woody hired a tutor. Yes, he really did, a private philosophy tutor to teach him the things his wife was learning at Hunter College. Trying to catch up. He felt a little guilty, you see, and a little inferior to all those college men and especially, college girls. Even though he was sometimes pulling down $1,500 a week as a comedy writer, he felt inferior. It just goes to show what an Old World upbringing will do for you.

The old inferiority sometimes surfaces, even now. Like when Woody explains about Lou Jacobi's kinky role in *Sex*.

"Please understand that he is not a fag, but a transvestite. The latter requires a college degree."

With all that guilt, Woody must feel terrific to see his stuff in the *New Yorker*. Whether accurately or not, the *New Yorker* has been called the most influential intellectual magazine in the country. One thing for sure, it's read by a lot of people with college degrees. And now, Woody Allen is read by a lot of people with college degrees. And they're laughing. B.A.'s and M.A.'s and even Ph.D's have become Woody Allen fans. What a way of getting even.

Not coincidentally, *Getting Even* was the title of Woody's first collection of prose pieces, mostly from the pages of the *New Yorker*. Of course, Woody has always wanted to be a "real" writer. Ever since he was a kid, he's wanted to write plays. But the first time he submitted a piece to the *New Yorker,* he was as nervous as a bride.

"They asked me if I'd consider rewriting the ending. They didn't know I'd do anything to have them print my stuff. I'd have made the ending into a hydrofoil if they'd wanted me to."

So what's he getting even for, exactly? For not having been to college, for not being an intellectual, for all those beatnik girls in the Village who put him down because he wasn't into weird poetry or nineteenth-century philosophers. How many of those guys he got dumped for, those skinny ones with beards and black turtlenecks, have been published by the *New Yorker*? By now, they probably all live in the burbs and own two Volkswagens and a mortgage. Maybe the most intellectual thing they do is subscribe to the *New Yorker*.

Well, he's getting even with the authors he does parodies of, too. He has a nerve, this joker with nothing except a high-school diploma, to make fun of heavies like Ingmar Bergman and Friederich Nietzsche. Most of his career, Woody's been making himself look bad. In his writing, though, he looks good. He's smarter than the smarties, because he's so good that he can do parodies of them. When Woody writes, he doesn't make fun of himself. Here, he's fully competent, the author, the boss.

During all the years when writers pictured Woody as an "intellectual" or a "cerebral" comedian, he was secretly embarrassed by those labels. It's not that he didn't want to be thought of as an egghead. He did. But he was sensitive to the fact that comedy, even though it's probably the most difficult kind of writing, is somehow an inferior form. He was stung by how unfair it was. Why should *Sleeper* or *City Lights*, be called trivial beside Antonioni or Eisenstein films?

Woody's talent is a comic talent. He's

always known it. He has to exercise his gift, or it'll go soft like an old football player's belly. For better or worse, he's a born funnyman. But he's still jealous of serious writers. So he seeks a small revenge on great artists, meaning people who aren't comedians. Woody laughs at them. "Them" means just about everyone, every writer around. He's made stylish fun of, among others, the Hasidic masters, Kafka, Dostoevsky, Freud, Bellow, Studs Terkel, and Ross MacDonald.

In fact, Woody ranges so widely among the things of this world, laughing all the way, that some people criticize him for taking nothing seriously. Never mind that comedians aren't *supposed* to take things seriously. They say Woody Allen won't last, that he'll never really be great, because nothing is sacred to him.

Well, what did Nichols and May take seriously? Can't think of a thing. Lenny Bruce? As soon as he started taking things seriously, he stopped being funny. Poor Woody has succeeded so completely, become such a favorite of the college set, that they're starting to roast him for being what he's always been, a joker. Ridiculous. Doesn't apply. What kind of clown is a serious clown, except a bore?

There is one thing Woody reveres, though, and that's his own comic talent. He's a slave to it. Every day, no matter what, he retires to his writing room. Exercise, you know, a workout for the old skills. He regards his gift as a responsibility, an idea that few people manage to live by, once they get famous. Another thing that Woody is keeping even with is his own potential. No matter what they say, he thinks being funny is a respectable skill, a kind of genius. He's not content with being funny. He'll be funnier. If Woody Allen is just a jester, he'll be the best there ever was.

"I don't care much about what the critics say," he tells you. Every star says that, of course, but when Woody says it, it's believable.

"If you're good, you know it. It doesn't matter how badly they pan you. And if you're bad, no amount of praise can change that, either. I'm my own worst critic, so there's nothing to be afraid of from the papers."

Who does Woody measure himself against, when he writes comedy? Only the best. Robert Benchley and S. J. Perelman, usually, plus boyhood idols like Max (Dobie Gilles) Shulman.

"When I first started to write parodies, I wrote like Shulman. As close as I possibly could get. Then, after I discovered Benchley and Perelman, I wrote like them. It's the best way to learn. From the masters."

He learned, he learned. There's something

of all of them in Woody's parodies now, as well as other comic writers he's run across since. When he first started, he submitted stuff to *Playboy* and *Esquire,* who gobbled it up like they were never going to get any more. They were right. Once Woody made it at the *New Yorker,* he dropped out of the dressed-up girlie mags.

Those early pieces were elaborations on Woody's nightclub routines. Sort of necklaces of one-line gags. For example, there was "Match Wits With Inspector Ford," in *Playboy.* This one was a parody of all the two-minute mysteries that used to appear in the *Saturday Evening Post.* The subtitle was "minute-and-three-quarter mysteries for the amateur sleuth and professional masochist," and the contents read like shaggy dog stories made up of series of quick gags. One victim of foul play was Clifford Wheel, who had been felled by a croquet mallet. Just before he died, Wheel had dipped his finger into the inkwell and scrawled, "Fall Sale Prices Drastically Reduced—Everything Must Go!" This message causes Wheel's servant, whose elevator shoes make him two inches shorter, to remark, "A businessman to the end." You get the idea. Each mystery ends with the answer to the puzzle in italics, headed, "How Did Inspector Ford Know?" Naturally, the answers are non sequiturs bearing little or no relation to the clues given.

Often the prose by-lined "Woody Allen" was nothing more than a series of captions written to accompany photographs of Woody with some starlet or other. Sometimes the photographic sessions were staged by Woody himself, which were invariably funnier than those staged by *Playboy*. In one such, Woody explains "Shindai, or the ancient, formal art of Japanese pillow fighting." Pictures show Woody and a very well-endowed and very tall lady in kimono whacking each other with pillows. Here are the beginnings of Woody Allen, the visual clown. Woody was less scrupulous about his research in those days. He clearly didn't know the difference between Japan and China. "Peking Duck, the Chinese dish, was originally a shindai term telling the man to duck and stop peeking. This was later changed to an order of Beef Lo-Mein." Still, the concept was funny. The parody, ragged in spots, suggested how good Woody would be when he'd tightened it up.

The best of Woody's pre-*New Yorker* pieces was his "Snow White," which appeared in *Playboy*. By this time the writing was considerably more like Robert Benchley than Max Shulman. "Snow White" is a coherent parody, hilarious in spots, of a straight theater review such as one done perhaps by Walter Kerr or Clive Barnes. Only here, the production under scrutiny is Elia Kazan's all-star *Snow White*, starring Marlon Brando,

Lee J. Cobb, Anthony Quinn, Jason Robards, Jr., Rod Steiger, George C. Scott and Sidney Poitier as the seven dwarfs.

Here, of course, Woody sets up a premise that holds possiblities for huge numbers of comic changes. He doesn't miss one. After soberly comparing Lee Cobb's Dopey to Sir Ralph Richardson's a few seasons ago, Woody goes on to evaluate the individual performances, squeezing the preposterous situation for all it's worth. Doc (Rod Steiger), we learn, is a hopeless alcoholic, "unable to 'whistle while he works.' " Sneezy (Robards) achoos neurotically because of his guilty feelings over having turned Happy in to the Nazis during World War II. And so on, through Brando's Sleepy, tormented by fears that "I'm not really as cute and cuddly as I think. Oh, sure, I'm tiny as could be and I got a little pointed hat. But I don't know—I just wish I was...more adorable." In the end we discover that the anti-Semitic Grumpy is really himself of Jewish extraction ("his mother...was seduced by a water sprite named Ben Fleagel, who promised her stockings"), and that the voice of the mirror is Walter Winchell's.

This is Woody Allen as mature comic writer. It reminds you of Benchley in pieces like "Opera Synopses," where he gives outlandish plots for various vaguely familiar operas such as "Lucy de Lima." If "Snow White" was

Benchley-inspired, it wouldn't be the first time. Like all serious writers, and humor is serious business, Woody is quick, even eager, to admit his influences. His first play, *Don't Drink the Water*, is clearly in imitation of Kaufman's *You Can't Take It with You*, and *Play It Again, Sam* also shows Kaufman's influence. As a director, Woody has allowed as how he learned things from Chaplin, Keaton, Truffaut, Robert Altman, Arthur Penn, Ingmar Bergman, Antonioni, Tati, Mike Nichols, and Eisenstein, to name a few.

As for comic writers whose work has left its mark on Woody's, he seems to be heading toward a syntheses of all the big ones. There's Shulman, of course, and Neil Simon, and maybe a bit of Noel Coward. But most of all, there's Benchley and S. J. Perelman, the only enduring comic essayists this country has produced in the last fifty years. He has not been especially influenced by Art Buchwald, Russell Baker, Dorothy Parker, or Ambrose Bierce, all of whom are more or less social satirists. Woody has always stayed notably clear of political reference in his work, perhaps because he can see in what happened to people like Mort Sahl that political humor has no staying power.

One writer who wasn't much like Woody is James Thurber. In technique and style, they are very different. Thurber, unlike both

Benchley and Perelman, was not a jokester. He was a master at building up a situation to that point when it teetered at the climax, uncertain whether to slide into comedy or poignance. Usually the weight tipped in favor of comedy, but not always. As critics and friends have often observed, Thurber was a pessimistic, even misanthropic man. His battles between the sexes, written as comedy, were dead serious for him throughout his adult life. This is also a serious matter for another comic pessimist, namely, Woody Allen. Woody does share with Thurber an underlying dourness that is largely absent in Benchley and Perelman. It's easy to imagine that if Fortune had not treated Woody Allen so well, as it did not James Thurber, he might easily have become the same kind of bitter guy.

But he has escaped bitterness, and remains the sort of humorist we can more easily take to our hearts—the mildly pessimistic parodist. The parodies reveal Woody at his most literate, moving away from the Allen comic persona to lampoon everything from the Mafia to the NYU catalogue. "A Look at Organized Crime," for example, is a cross between *The Valachi Papers* and a *Village Voice* expose. In this piece, Allen reveals for the first time that the *Cosa Nostra* is staffed by guys with names like Gaetano Santucci (also known as Little Tony or Rabbi Henry

Sharpstein), Kid Lipsky, Albert (The Logical Positivist) Corillo, and Little Petey (Big Petey) Ross. We also hear about, "Irish Larry Doyle—a racketeer so suspicious that he refused to let anybody in New York ever get behind him, and walked down the street constantly pirouetting and spinning around."

Early in his writing career, Woody's taste in names ran to the baroque. There were Victor Shakopolis and Fielding Mellish, of course, not to mention Gossage, Vardebedian, Quincy Freem, Kermit Kroll and Kaiser Lupowitz. This fondness for highly descriptive names has been likened to Perelman's, though Woody's names seem tame beside some of Perelman's. Witness Noreen Cannister, Max Bibulous (her wealthy lover), Patrick Foley de Grandeur, and his accountant, Tony Fiduciari. Perelman, like Allen, seems to feel that ethnic names are automatically amusing, and Armenian names are hilarious. Perelman manages to drop a Bazurdjian or a Harootunian into nearly every one of his pieces. On their behalf, it should be said that both Allen and Perelman make fun of Jewish names as much if not more than any other group. And Perelman, who has been at it a bit longer than Woody, manages to zero in on those un-traceable American names like Walt Zymchuck and Edward Gipf.

You know when you read Woody Allen's comic essays that he is very familiar with both Benchley and Perelman. Not that he imitates, strictly speaking, but he has studied and used most of the tricks. Some have worked for him better than others. Perelman's ornate, slithery diction—gladioli and onions—can be imitated, but can hardly be outdone. Nobody alive except Perelman could have pulled off a sentence like, "If you have no further questions, Miss Cronjager, it is incumbent on me to scoot." Nor is there anyone with Perelman's virtuoso vocabulary: "I have shorn all his highflown rodomontade, euphuistical bombast, and sesquipedalian twaddle and distilled tales comprehensible to the veriest moron, to the most benighted redneck, to even a rock fan." This is the sort of stuff that is so beautiful when it works, and it always works for Perelman, that it makes you want to sit right down at the typewriter and bat out a few. As they say, he makes it look easy.

Woody Allen is a careful reader, just as he is a careful everything else. You can tell he's given a lot of thought to how Perelman gets his magic mix of words from the Oxford Unabridged, words from the corner bar, and words from right out of left field, or maybe the moon. Yet, when Woody tries it, most prominently in a piece from *Getting Even* called, "A Little Louder, Please," there is something labored about the whole business. Take this mouthful, for instance, an obvious case of

Perelmania: "Also laddies, as one whose spate of insights first placed *Godot* in proper perspective for the many confused playgoers who milled sluggishly in the lobby during intermission, miffed at ponying up scalper's money for argle-bargle bereft of one up-tune or a single spangled bimbo, I would have to say my rapport with the seven livelies is pretty solid."

Good Perelman, but not great Perelman, and certainly not as good as Perelman's Perelman. The trouble with this as a Perelman parody is that Perelman's own stuff is both funnier and more outrageous. In spite of Woody's clear consciousness of all his subject's favorite devices, especially the long delay in finally coming to the point of the essay ("I digress," said Max Shulman), you have the sense not so much of reading a joke at Perelman's expense as of reading a forgery. In this one, at least, Woody doesn't quite get even.

The Ross MacDonald parodies, on the other hand, are superb, particularly "The Whore of Mensa." Both this one and "Mr. Big," from the *Getting Even* collection, play on what might be called MacDonald's intellectual pretensions, or at least his aspiration to be taken more seriously than your average detective-story hack. In "Mr. Big," Kaiser Lupowitz, the hard-boiled Lew Archer figure with the sentimental soft center, is hired to investigate the existence and subsequent death of God. On the trail of Mr. Big, Kaiser consults a rabbi who is sure of the deity's existence, though not allowed to pronounce His name.

"You ever see Him?" asks Kaiser.

"Me? Are you kidding? I'm lucky I get to see my grandchildren."

"Then how do you know He exists?"

"How do I know? What kind of question is that? Could I get a suit like this for fourteen dollars if there was no one up there? Here, feel a gabardine—how can you doubt?"

In the end, Kaiser figures out that God was done in by his client, an academic with bleached blond hair who goes under the (assumed) name of Heather Butkiss. He confronts her with his suspicions.

"Kaiser, you're mad!"

"No, baby. You posed as a pantheist and that gave you access to Him—*if* He existed, which he did. He went with you to Shelby's party and when Jason wasn't looking, you killed Him."

"Who the hell are Shelby and Jason?"

"What's the difference? Life's absurd now, anyway."

The story ends with blood and revealed meaning, which is standard for Lew Archer and Kaiser Lupowitz. "The Whore of Mensa" has a similar finish, and an even funnier concept, in which Kaiser exposes a call-girl ring that specializes in intellectual discussions. He rings up the madame.

"I'd like to discuss Melville."

"*Moby Dick* or the shorter novels?"

"What's the difference?"

"The price. That's all. Symbolism's extra."

In this piece, Woody catches not only the detective-fiction rhythm and rattling dialogue, but the rather subtle character of the suspicious and sympathetic Archer, a private eye who can never quite decide whether he's literate or not. When Kaiser tells the girl from the intellectual brothel that he's a cop ("I'm fuzz, sugar, and discussing Melville for money is an 802"), she breaks down. Kaiser melts. He knows her type. "She was every dame you saw waiting in line at the Elgin or the Thalia, or penciling the words, 'Yes, very true' into the margin of some book on Kant." (The Elgin and the Thalia are once-and-future art movie houses in New York, yet another example of Woody's penchant for home-town references. Unlike Woody and Kaiser, Lew Archer is most at home in Southern California.)

Woody has always been better when the joke is up front; when he starts from a patently preposterous situation—"The Moose

Mingles" sort of thing—than when his premise is a more subtle magnification of reality like Perelman's. That's why the Ross MacDonald parodies are funnier. There's more than one way to juxtapose incongruities, and Woody's way has usually been to bash them until they clang. He is not, like Thurber, one of those humorists who sneaks up on you. There are exceptions, of course, nice little touches in among the body blows. In his parody of the college catalogue, for instance, he describes, "Introduction of Psychology: The theory of human behavior. Why some men are called, 'lovely individuals' and why there are others you just want to pinch." But mostly it's the broad brush that Woody wields best, his traditional tool.

Perhaps this explains why Woody seems most at home working within the frame of explicit parody. In his "Death Knocks," he burlesques Bergman's *The Seventh Seal* and it's famous metaphysical chess game. Only when the writer is Woody Allen, the game is gin rummy. Nat Ackerman, a dress manufacturer and all-around *schlep*, is visited by Death, who turns out to be an even bigger *schlep*. Nat is anxious to live because his firm has just merged with Modiste Originals. But, and this is where comic fantasy has it all over Bergman, Nat Ackerman beats Death at his own game. ("Do I play gin rummy?" says Death. "Is Paris a city?") Death bothers Woody Allen even more than it bothers the rest of us, because he's always thinking about it. Here, in the person of Nat Ackerman, he approaches it under cover of comedy, and is depressed by what he sees. Death is so banal. He deserves to lose. If only he would, just once. How Nat and Woody and we would like it to be different. Nat says, "What's it like?"

"*Death*: 'What's what like?' [Throughout the following, they pick and discard.]

"*Nat*: 'Death.'

"*Death*: 'What should it be like? You lay there.'

"*Nat*: 'Is there anything after?'

"*Death*: 'Aha, you're saving twos.'

"*Nat*: 'I'm asking. Is there anything after?'

"*Death*: '(absently): You'll see.'

"*Nat*: 'Oh, then I will actually see something?'

"*Death*: 'Well, maybe I shouldn't have put it that way. Throw.' " Or, as Nietzsche would have said if Woody Allen had been writing his material, "Eternal nothingness is O.K., if you're dressed for it."

Death is everywhere in Woody Allen's comic writing, popping up with a self-propelled insistence that recalls Bergman much more than either Benchley or Perelman.

In, "A Guide to Some of the Lesser Ballets," clearly modeled on Benchley, there is this abrupt finish to "A Day in the Life of a Doe:" "A fawn dances on and nibbles slowly at some leaves. He drifts lazily through the soft foliage. Soon he starts coughing and drops dead." You wouldn't catch Robert Benchley doing such a thing to Lucy de Lima. You might catch Woody Allen learning a little restraint from Benchley, though, to temper his Perelmanesque excesses; just as he seems to be using Buster Keaton's influence in his films to dilute an excess of Chaplin. "A Guide" is even a little more subtle than Benchley's "Opera Synopses," or maybe it's just that times have changed. The Benchley piece was written in 1922, when you could get away with calling an Italian opera parody, "Il Minnestrone."

Benchley was an advocate of a humorous technique he called "The Blind Explanation," or the answer that obfuscates twice as much as it clarifies. His own classic example was, "There is no such place as Budapest." Another example from Benchley: "A crowd of sightseers and villagers is present. Roger appears, looking for Laura. He can not find her. Laura appears, looking for Roger. She can not find him." You should understand that we, the reader, have never heard of Roger and Laura before, nor will they be mentioned again.

The Blind Explanation. There is little doubt that Woody has mastered this technique, after his own fashion: "Men and women sit in separate groups and then begin to dance, but they have no idea why and soon sit down again." Or a one-liner he uses frequently: "All literature is a footnote to Faust. I have no idea what I mean by that." The B.E. has proved especially useful to Woody in his parodies of dreams, a difficult stunt for a man whose writing is like dreams to begin with. Here's a dream-sentence from, "Notes from the Overfed," written, he says, after reading Dostoevsky and *Weight Watcher's Magazine* on the same plane trip. "I become [in the dream] hysterical with laughter, which suddenly turns to tears and then into a serious ear infection." You can always tell that you're in the presence of a Blind Explanation by the urge you feel to say, "Wha?"

Benchley, of course, could turn social satirist on occasion, and could also display some of the xenophobia that has characterized even the most cosmopolitan of American humorists. In a 1925 essay titled, "French for Americans," Benchley gave this table for pronunciation of the French vowels:

Vowels	Pronounced
a	ong
e	ong
i	ong
o	ong
u	ong

Like Woody Allen, Benchley and Perelman
are basically New Yorkers, feeding on the
cadence of New York speech, and the propen-
sity of the New York mind to crack wise. In the
matter of names, Benchley was more restrained than either Allen or Perelman. In his
casting of mock-Italian opera, for example, he
forces himself to refrain from the more
flagrant violations of Italian-American
friendship, resting content with naming his
rude mechanicals Cleanso, Turino, and Bom-
bo. Woody, on the other hand, is responsible
for such Italian-Americans as Anthony (The
Fish) Rotunno. Lately, Woody's names have
begun to be less descriptive and heavily
onomatopoeic, more amusing and subtle. He
seems to be shooting for a Benchley-like
atmosphere, where the names themselves are
not the jokes, but contribute in a less obtrusive
way to the good humor of the piece. Recent
names of this kind include Quincy Marple,
Achille Londos, the noted Greek psychic, and
Mr. J. C. Dubbs. Still, Woody is not above

throwing in a Dr. Osgood Mulford Twelge to relieve the subtlety.

The parodies themselves have been of a more subtle nature since the publication of *Getting Even.* One, called "No Kaddish for Weinstein," is a gentle, mocking piece about one of those modern Jewish types you find in the work of Saul Bellow or the early Philip Roth. Weinstein, like Augie March, had been a precocious boy, "An intellectual. At twelve, he had translated the poems of T. S. Eliot into English, after some vandals had broken into the library and translated them into French." Like poor Portnoy, Weinstein has trouble with sex and Jewish women: " 'It's no damn good with you, Harriet,' he used to complain. 'You're too pure. Every time I have an urge for you, I sublimate it by planting a tree in Israel. You remind me of my mother.' " His relationship with his divorced wife is one of mutually dependent obtuseness. " 'Hello, Harriet,' he said.

" 'Oh, Ike,' she said. 'You needn't be so damn self-righteous.'

"She was right. What a tactless thing to have said. He hated himself for it."

The sensibilities of Bellow and especially of Roth are perfectly familiar to Woody Allen. The Little Drip is almost like a two-dimensional Neil Klugman, the post-adolescent lover in *Goodby, Columbus*, torn between his intelligence and his desire to sell out for fun and profit. Roth, before he flipped, was a truly substantial comic writer in a way that Woody Allen can't be, unless he somehow learns to create characters.

But Woody, in his way, seems to be moving closer to an honest vision of the one character he does understand, himself. The fact that he is able to combine honesty with comedy is what makes his writing increasingly popular with the "intellectuals" who read the *New Yorker*. Woody is already a long way from *What's New, Pussycat*, and opening more distance every day.

To see how far Woody's humor has come since the cabaret days, look at how he reworks an old routine for publication as a prose piece. "A Twenties Memory," from *Getting Even*, was originally published in the *Chicago Daily News* as, "How I Became a Comedian," and is based on a routine Woody was doing in clubs in 1965.

"I was in Europe many years ago, with Ernest Hemingway," he would say, and pause for the inevitable laugh. "Hemingway had just written his first novel. Gertrude Stein and I read it. We said it was a good novel, but not a great one, that it needed some work, but it could be a fine book. We laughed over it, and Hemingway punched me in the mouth."

Here's how the same material comes out

after being filtered through the sophistication of the older Woody.

"I first came to Chicago in the twenties, and that was to see a fight. Ernest Hemingway was with me and we both stayed at Jack Dempsey's training camp. Hemingway had just finished two short stories about prize fighting, and while Gertrude Stein and I both thought they were decent, we agreed they still needed much work. I kidded Hemingway about his forthcoming novel and we laughed a lot and had fun and then we put on some boxing gloves and he broke my nose."

It's the same stuff, really. Woody Allen as a member of the Lost Generation, hobnobbing with Picasso and Joyce and Hemingway and Stein. But the later material, the writing, is so much better informed—more grown-up. This little turn, for instance, appears only in the written work, not in the club act:

"Picasso's studio was so unlike Matisse's in that, while Picasso's was sloppy, Matisse kept everything in perfect order. Oddly, enough, just the reverse was true."

What?

Here's another one: "Gris was provincially Spanish, and Gertrude Stein used to say that only a true Spaniard could behave as he did; that is, he would speak Spanish and sometimes return to his family in Spain. It was really quite marvelous to see."

What Woody chose to leave out when he

reworked his old jokes is as revealing as what he put in. This was dropped:

"Scott (Fitzgerald) had just written *Great Expectations*. Gertrude Stein and I read it, and we said it was a good book, but there was no need to have written it, 'cause Charles Dickens had already written it. We laughed over it, and Hemingway punched me in the mouth."

In *Getting Even*, instead of writing *Great Expectations*, Scott and Zelda have been asked by Grant Wood to pose for "American Gothic." During the sitting, Scott keeps dropping his pitchfork.

Comparing the two routines, you get the impression that Woody has loosened up a lot over the years. He's more relaxed, and he manages to catch more of the flavor of the period and the people.

"Writing is the easiest thing I do. There's nobody to please but myself."

No audience. No sea of expectant faces. No obligation to knock 'em dead. No wonder he's more relaxed. Less hostile, too. To Woody, sitting alone with his typewriter is a vacation, a goof.

He's gotten just a bit more goofy in recent years. Maybe success is a good tranquilizer. For a star, Woody still runs pretty hard, but nobody could keep up the pace he had in the early sixties. He has more fun now, does what he wants to do more often. Pleases himself first. Not that he doesn't still go for the laughs. Even in his writing, he reaches mostly for one-line effects. The audience isn't there, but Woody is such an expert at turning the folks on that he *knows* what they'd laugh at.

"I'm not exactly a novelist. I just do these little parodies. I do them for fun. I'd love to write like Benchley or Perelman. I admire them both *tremendously*. Well, you know, I'd like to write a novel, too. Because there aren't many funny ones any more. And I think I could do a long piece and make it funny. That's for between movies. That's for fun."

You can see, when you read Woody's parodies, that he's starting to reach beyond his own personality. Yes, the spotlight is still on a Woody-figure, but not all the time, like it used to be. One of his biggest faults as a writer and performer is that he never gives any *personality* to any characters except the Little Drip.

"That's right, I guess," he says, acknowledging the criticism. "But look at Groucho. Look at Fields. Do you remember them as actors, performing off of other characters, or as solitary comic personalities? They were essentially loners, like me."

But Woody the Writer knows that if he's

really going to do a novel, he'll have to learn character. He's working at it. Look at his magazine stuff. Look at his most recent scripts. Even in *Sleeper*, we're starting to see some real people. Diane Keaton, playing the future-poet Luna, is very close to a second lead. A real person.

"Diane is a very strong actress," says her friend. "So is Louise. They're great. You just leave them alone. They *create* character. It doesn't have to be written for them."

As it stands, there are two Woodies. Number one is still pretty much of a gag man. A boomer. An incessantly performing grotesque. This is still the most popular Woody, the one that makes audiences start laughing as soon as he appears on screen or on stage, before he even says a word. This is the Woody of visual *schtick*. The clothes and hair and expression never change. He's recognized on the street. Kids run up to him in the park, look up into his face, and say, "Hey, Mr. Allen, is that really you?" He gets sick of it. He loves it. It's what he was working for all those years in the saloons, but sometimes it drives him crazy.

"I don't wear disguises. Just my rainhat, pulled down over the top of my face, and my collar turned up over the bottom. I mean, I can't go around in a blond wig and elevator shoes. I'd look like Mrs. Nixon."

The other Woody looks the same, except you never see him. He comes alive only in the writing room. He appears only in print. He keeps the kind of hours we associate with corporation executives and speed freaks. To people interested in that sort of thing, Woody Number Two is known as a serious practitioner of the comic art. Critics have started to compare his movie direction to the best: Chaplin, Keaton. His writing has drawn mostly praise. The most cutting criticism he gets is that he's "sophomoric." To Woody, who flunked out in his freshman year, it's a compliment.

What can we expect to see in the future from the creator of Kaiser Lupowitz and Ike Weinstein?

"I want to do more subtle stuff. More ordinary situations, less really outlandish stuff. That can be funny, too. In fact, when you do it right, it's funnier than science fiction. It might turn out that I'm best at the broader things. But I'm not ready to admit it until I've tried. You can't stand still."

That's his motto. He never stands still. Even when he's supposedly sitting and writing, he's really walking the floor, wearing out the rug, jittering and jiving and telling his jokes out loud to himself. It's dark outside. It's that time of night when sensible people are in bed and crazy guys, like Woody, get their best work done. There is one lamp burning over the typewriter as the camera pans back and up, out of the room...Light pours down on the writer's chair, but Woody isn't in it. Suddenly, he steps into the spot, looking up with his unmistakable quizzical expression.

Interviewer: What makes you work so hard, Woody? Who are you trying to catch?

Woody: What? Oh, um, there are lots of people I look up to. (He sets his jaw in a determined line.) I got lotsa heroes.

Interviewer: Who are they, Woody? Who do you want to emulate?

Woody: Great performers. My true heroes are Frank Sinatra and Fatty Arbuckle.

The camera moves away until Woody is standing alone, a little figure in a spotlight, surrounded by a sea of black. Soundtrack under, with the sound of a single, softly laughing voice.

Interviewer: Frank Sinatra and Fatty Arbuckle. Right. Thanks a lot for your time, Mr. Allen.

Laughter up and out.

Goodnight, Woody. Thanks for everything.

THE GREAT WOODY ALLEN TRIVIA TEST

The Answers, (more or less)

Photo No. 1 was taken on a rainy afternoon in the early 1970s by an unidentified photographer in a raincoat, using a Hasselblad and Tri-X film. *No. 2*...by another unidentified lensman, taken between takes on the set of the film, *Sleeper*, 1973. Copyright United Artists Corp. *No. 3*...at home, November, 1966, tooting on his pet clarinet. UPI photo. *No. 4* answering questions for the press, New York, June, 1975. *Love and Death* was about to open. UPI photo. *No. 5*...one of his early 8″x10″ glossies. A 1963 portrait by Maurice Seymour of New York. *No. 6*...he went *Bananas* in July of 1971; writing, directing, and starring in the film. Wide World photo. *No. 7*...courtesy of a friend. *No. 8*...schlepping at shortstop for the Broadway League, June, 1969. *No. 9*... *What's New, Pussycat?* Or, why else would I walk around in this costume. *No. 10*...at home, putting together a chocolate malted. New York, 1966. UPI photo. *No. 11*...*Play It Again, Sam*. "But it's my move, my movie, and get your eyes off my Coors!" A Paramount Picture, 1972. *No. 12*...same movie, different view. *No. 13*...back to *Bananas*, 1971. Remember the shower bit? *No. 14*...*Love and Death*, 1975, a United Artists film. That's death on the right. *No. 15*...feeling good in *Sleeper*, 1973. *No. 16*...at the mercy of the court, *Bananas*. *No.*

17...on location near San Juan, July, 1970, it's *Bananas* again. Wide World photo. *No. 18*...would you believe *Sleeper*? *No. 19*...How about *Bananas* again, mammy. *No. 20*...Woody and his Broadway cast of *Play It Again, Sam*, January, 1969. The other guy is Tony Roberts. The girls are (clockwise, from left) Barbara Press, Diane Keaton, Jean Fowler, Lee Ann Fahey, Sheila Sullivan, Patti Caton, Barbara Brownell, Cynthia Dalbey, Diana Walker. Wide World photo. *No. 21*...*Play It Again, Sam*, again, this time it's the film. *No. 22*...one of the bunch from *Bananas*. *No. 23*...*Love and Death*, "and why do they keep interrupting us?" *No. 24*...*Love and Death*, "and me and this big mouth." *No. 25*...*What's New Pussycat*? *No. 26*...the courageous commuter in, yes, *Bananas*. *No. 27*...*Love and Death*, guess which one is the star swordsman? *No. 28*...*Sleeper*. *No. 29*...*Play It Again, Sam*, "only this time do it my way. I'm the boss." *No. 30*...*Play It Again, Sam*. Throwing around dough like it was bread. *No. 31*...*Play It Again, Sam*. Woody plays it again. *No. 32*...It's a banana, but it's in *Sleeper*. *No. 33*...*Love and Death*, as any cossack knows. *No. 34*...*Bananas*. *No. 35*...*Bananas*, again, Sam. Courtesy of *Movie Star News*. *No. 36*...*Play It Again Sam*, but easy on the trenchcoat.

Now, that wasn't too hard. Here's the tough part. And the first reader with the correct answers gets an autographed copy of this book. Who's the girl in photo No. 12? Who's the guy in photo No. 13? What was Woody's line in photo No. 18? What happened next in photo No. 23? Why is Woody called *Woody*?